Beach Cuisine

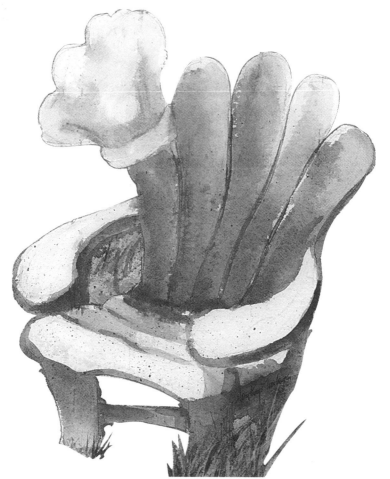

**A Collection of Recipes
From the Atlantic Coast.**
by Jewel Cammarano

*I dedicate this book to all who love
awaking to the sound of the sea,
smelling the sweet ocean air, feeling
one's feet in the sand and viewing
a Carolina sunset.*

03 02 01 00 / 10 9 8 7 6 5 4 3 2

Manufactured in the United States of America

FATHER & SON

PUBLISHING, INC.

4909 N. Monroe Street
Tallahassee, Florida 32303
http://www.fatherson.com

Introduction

The Coastline stretched forever—a barrier island visibly separated from the mainland by miles of sand and water and estuaries in many directions. The colors of bright golden sands, green indigenous beach growth and endless shades of blue water, darkening in hue as the ocean swept into the depths away from the mainland and blended into the sky.

So was my impression of an aerial photograph, published in National Geographic Magazine those many, many years ago. The coastline of North Carolina, referred to as "The Outer Banks," in the early 70's, was a place of sheer and unspoiled, natural beauty. A magical coastline that I had to see!

Our first vacation there, with our young children was a revelation. Accommodations were few in number and modest at best. Activities were limited to fishing, swimming and birdwatching at most, and the few local restaurants offered selections of regional fare—a bounty of seafood fresh from the local waters, the freshest vegetables and herbs a warm climate and rich soil could produce. A cuisine one might adeptly describe as "down-home-cooking" and a cuisine that was totally new to all of us. But it was a special feeling when I left—that took me years to describe—that would bring me back again and again, and finally make me stay.

For several summers following, we explored further south all of the places we could find along that coast. We trekked our way through North and South Carolina, not missing a view. Vistas of sand and sea and sunshine so beautiful they could take your breath away. Quaint and charming fishing villages with their lay-back life-styles allowed one to get lost in the relaxation of it all; and historical homes and sites could bring you back one, two or three hundred years, if you chose. But always, and everywhere in the South, was the cuisine—so steeped in Southern tradition and influenced by all the cultures that settled on these lands —so impressive to me. I was in love!

They came by boat and they came by wooden bridges. Geographically isolated and accessible only by boat until the first bridges were constructed in the 1930's, many of the coastal regions of the Carolina's were sought by many as their getaway. Wealthy families came to spend summers, bringing with them whole extended families and staff. More adventurous souls sought rugged and deserted beaches for their campsites. They came for the sun and they came for the sea; and most of all, they came just to be— just to be a family. They brought with them dreams and "hopes of mind and bone, of the best days yet to be."* They brought their culture, their supplies and their cuisine.

And so we came. We came back to the place of our very first visit—a small village called "Duck"—that had captured my heart completely. We were blessed that day as we stood on a dune, surrounded by bright blue sky and a panoramic view of ocean, sand and sound. We had found our place — a place surrounded by wild bird refuge; a place where wild horses roamed and only the adventurous could travel further north in their four-wheel drives. We had found the site on which we would build a beach house, a place we would return to year after year and spend times in our lives we would always remember; times that would always be so special to all of us. I thanked the Lord for creating such a pristine and magnificent landscape and allowing us to share it. For that we did.

The years that followed brought endless days of joyous gatherings. Family, friends and friends of family, casts of thousands coming "just to be." Sun, sand, sea and camaraderie were always on the menu—and that always meant one thing to me—how do I feed this hungry crowd?

And so my book began.

*"HIGH DUNE" Duck, NC 1984

4

Table of Contents

Acknowledgements

To John, my husband and the love of my life, my gratitude for his encouragement and support, which has always been behind me in anything I have ever wanted to do. And I am especially grateful for his appetite.

To my children—whose love and pride in their mother have made me who I am.

To my family and friends, with whom over the years, and for all occasions, we have celebrated many of the recipes in this book.

To our customers, who come from all over and who have come back again and again, to seek out new recipes and share with us some of their own.

ABOUT THE AUTHOR: Jewel received a Bachlor of Science degree in Home Economics and Nutritional Science from the University of Connecticut. Before moving to Kitty Hawk, North Carolina where she presently resides with her husband, she taught Foods and Nutrition in several states. She has owned and operated two gourmet gift shops for ten years on the Outer Banks. When not inventing recipes in the kitchen, she loves playing golf and gardening. The largest loves of her life are the grandchildren presented to her by her two children.

Cover art by Mary Kay Umberger, free-lance artist and owner of her own gallery in Corolla, North Carolina.

Appetizers & Beverages

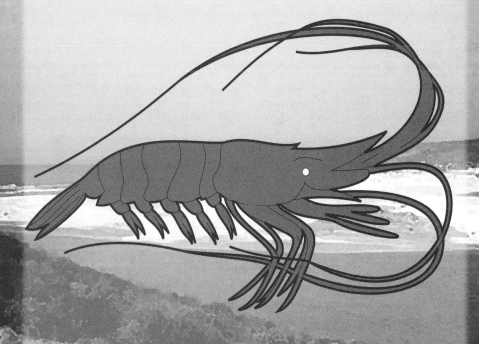

Appetizers & Beverages

ARTICHOKE DIP

1   14-ounce jar artichoke hearts, drained and quartered
½   cup sour cream
½   cup mayonnaise
1   small bunch green onions, chopped
1   tablespoon fresh lemon juice
1   clove garlic, minced
     salt and pepper to taste

Mix all ingredients together in a medium bowl. Transfer to a serving bowl and refrigerate overnight for the flavors to blend. Serve with pitas or crackers. Yield: 2 cups.

BARBECUED BACON-SHRIMP SKEWERS

1   pound large shrimp (20-24 count)
½   tablespoon Cajun seasoning
2   tablespoons barbecue sauce
4   ounces sliced bacon (about 6 slices)

Peel and devein shrimp, leaving tails intact; then butterfly them by cutting halfway through each shrimp along outside curve. Place in medium bowl; add Cajun seasoning. Toss to coat. Add barbecue sauce; stir to coat. Let sit 30 minutes.

Open shrimp; place cut side up on work surface. With a knife, quarter each slice of bacon crosswise. Cover each shrimp with a piece of bacon. Thread each on a 6-8" bamboo skewer, bacon side up. Place skewers bacon side up on wire rack in broiler pan; avoid crowding. Broil 3 inches from heat 5 minutes or until shrimp are cooked and bacon browns. Serve hot. Makes 8-10 servings.

BBQ CHICKEN & CHEDDAR QUESADILLAS

8	flour tortillas
1	4-ounce can chopped mild chilies
2	cups shredded BBQ chicken
½	cup shredded X-sharp Cheddar cheese
½	cup bottled taco sauce
	cilantro for garnish
1	cup bottled salsa
¼	cup sour cream

Heat oven to 450 degrees. Place one tortilla on large baking sheet. Spread with 1 tablespoon chilies. Top with one quarter of chicken, cheese and taco sauce. Place tortilla on top. Repeat with remaining tortillas, chiles, chicken, cheese, and sauce, for a total of 4 separate quesadillas. Bake for eight minutes, until crispy and cheese has melted. Remove from oven, let stand for 5 minutes. Cut into quarters. Garnish with cilantro, salsa and sour cream. Serves 8.

BOGUE INLET HERBED CHEESE BALL

2	(8-ounce) packages cream cheese, softened
1	tablespoon minced onion
1	(.4 ounce) package ranch salad dressing mix
1	cup chopped pecans

Combine cream cheese, minced onion and salad dressing in a mixing bowl. Beat at medium speed until smooth. Cover and chill several hours. Shape mixture into a ball, and roll in pecans. Serve with assorted crackers. Yield: 2 cups.

BOURSIN CHEESE SPREAD

1   (8-ounce) package lightly salted whipped butter, room temperature
2   (8-ounce) packages cream cheese, room temperature
1   teaspoon oregano
½   teaspoon garlic powder
¼   teaspoon thyme
¼   teaspoon marjoram
¼   teaspoon dill weed
¼   teaspoon coarsely ground pepper
¼   teaspoon basil
¼   teaspoon chervil
2   tablespoons freeze-dried chives
assorted crackers

With an electric mixer, blend all ingredients in a large bowl, at medium speed. Refrigerate at least 24 hours before serving, to blend flavors. Twenty minutes before serving, remove from refrigerator, and allow to stand at room temperature. Serve with crackers. Will keep several weeks in the refrigerator. Yield: 3 cups.

CLAM (OR OYSTER) FRITTERS

12   clams (or shucked oysters) in their liquor
3   eggs
1   cup whole milk
¾   cup flour, combined with
¼   cup seafood breader (seasoned)
     canola oil for frying

Drain clams (or oysters); remove shell particles; strain liquor and re-serve. Chop clams (oysters); refrigerate all.

Two hours before preparing, separate egg yolks from whites. Beat each separately; the yolks until thick and light yellow, the whites until stiff.
In a large mixing bowl, blend egg yolks, milk and clam (oyster) liquor; fold in whites; sift in enough flour-breader combo to make a thin batter. Add chopped clams (oysters); cover and refrigerate for 2 hours.

When ready to fry, heat oil in skillet over high flame. Do not allow to smoke. Fry spoonfuls of batter, a few at a time, in hot oil for 3 minutes, or until golden brown. Serve piping hot with tarter sauce. Serves 4-6.

CRAB FLAKE COCKTAIL

1   pint cooked, fresh crabmeat
3   tablespoons orange juice
1   grapefruit
4   tablespoons catsup
½   teaspoon Worcestershire sauce
     lettuce leaves

Purchase freshly cooked crab meat. Peel and cut grapefruit sections into small pieces and set aside. In a small bowl, blend orange juice, catsup and Worcestershire sauce. Line well-chilled cocktail glasses or sherbet cups with lettuce leaves. Fill with generous portion of crab mixture, place grape-fruit on top and pour orange juice mixture over all. Serve with saltines or Melba toast. Serves 4.

CURRITUCK CRAB DIP

1   package (8 ounce) cream cheese, softened
¼   cup light cream
2   teaspoons lemon juice
1½   teaspoons Worcestershire sauce
½   pound white crab meat, cooked
      dash salt & pepper

Stir cream cheese until smooth. Gradually add cream. Stir in lemon juice and Worcestershire sauce. Carefully, toss crab meat into mixture so as not to break up lumps. Season with salt and pepper. Chill. Yield: 1 ½ cups.

CURRY DIP

1   cup mayonnaise
1   cup low-fat plain yogurt
3   tablespoons ketchup
2   tablespoons grated onion
1   clove garlic, minced
1   tablespoon curry powder
1   tablespoon Worcestershire
1   teaspoon tabasco
      pinch salt

In a medium bowl, blend together the mayonnaise, yogurt and ketchup. Stir in the grated onion, garlic, curry powder, Worcestershire and tabasco. Season with a pinch of salt to taste. Serve over fresh, crispy veggies. Makes 2 cups.

DILLY VEGETABLE DIP

1   cup sour cream
1   (8-ounce) package cream cheese, softened
1   tablespoon chives, chopped
1   tablespoon parsley, chopped
1   teaspoon dried onion flakes
1   teaspoon dried dill
     salt to taste
½   teaspoon Worcestershire sauce
     dash tabasco sauce

Blend sour cream and cream cheese together in a medium bowl. Add herbs and spices, Worcestershire and Tabasco; blend well. Refrigerate until ready to serve. Goes well with crackers, chips or fresh-cut vegetables. Yield: about 2 cups.

FRESH PEACH SALSA

1   cup chopped fresh or frozen (thawed) peaches
1   cup chopped fresh tomato, seeded
¼   cup finely chopped red bell pepper
2   tablespoons finely chopped green onions
2 - 4 tablespoons grapefruit juice
4   teaspoons chopped fresh cilantro
     dash of salt

Mix all ingredients in a nonmetal bowl. Cover and refrigerate at least 1 hour to blend all flavors. Yield: about 2 ½ cups salsa.

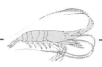

GUACAMOLE

2	medium-sized ripe avocados
1	tablespoon lime juice
1	medium onion, diced
1	ripe tomato, diced
1	clove garlic, crushed
½	teaspoon chili powder
	salt and pepper to taste
	tabasco or other hot sauce (optional)

Peel avocados, remove seeds, and mash in a bowl, using fork or a potato masher. Add lime juice, onion, tomato, garlic and chile powder, stirring them in thoroughly. Add salt and pepper to taste, and 2-3 drops of desired hot sauce to spice it up. Refrigerate until serving.

HATTERAS HOT CLAM DIP

1	(8-ounce) package cream cheese, softened
2	tablespoons sour cream
2	tablespoons mayonnaise
½	teaspoon onion powder
1	(6-ounce) can clams, drained
	Parmesan cheese
	fresh parsley, chopped

Preheat oven to 325 degrees. Spray an 8 or 9-inch pie plate with vegetable cooking spray. Mix cream cheese, sour cream, mayonnaise and onion powder together in a medium bowl. Toss to gently blend. Add clams and blend once more. Spread clam mixture evenly into the pie plate and sprinkle heavily with Parmesan cheese. Bake for 30 minutes, and top with chopped parsley. Serve with crackers. Serves 8-10.

HOME BAKED PITA CHIPS

1   package pita bread (about 6)
1   clove garlic, finely chopped
3   tablespoons olive oil

Heat oven to 375 degrees. Cut pitas in half to form semicircles; pull each apart into 2 separate pieces.

In a small bowl, stir together garlic and oil. Using a pastry brush, brush rough (inner) side of each piece of bread very lightly with oil mixture. Stack all of the pita pieces; cut into thirds, forming wedge shapes. Spread out in single layer on a large baking sheet.

Bake in 375 degrees oven 8 to 10 minutes or until crispy and golden brown. Serve warm with dips. Yield: 8-10 servings.

HOT CRAB MEAT SPREAD

1   (8-ounce) package cream cheese, softened
¼   cup milk
1   (6-ounce) can crab meat, drained and flaked
1   teaspoon horseradish
1   teaspoon Worcestershire sauce
¼   teaspoon salt
      paprika and chopped parsley for garnish

In a medium bowl, with an electric mixer, beat cheese with milk until smooth. Add crab meat, horseradish, Worcestershire and salt, mix thoroughly. Spread on firm crackers and bake on ungreased cookie sheet in a 350 degree oven for about 8 minutes. Sprinkle with paprika and garnish with parsley. Makes about 24.

KITTY HAWK MEXICAN PIZZA

2   10-inch flour tortillas
1   cup Monterey Jack cheese, shredded (4 ounces)
1   cup Cheddar cheese, shredded (4 ounces)
3   tablespoons sliced green onion
1   medium tomato, chopped
2   tablespoons green chili pepper, diced

Preheat oven to 350 degrees. Place the tortillas on a lightly greased baking sheet or pizza pan. Sprinkle cheeses evenly over the 2 tortillas. Top each with tomato, onion, and chili peppers. Bake about 5 minutes, or till cheese is bubbly. Remove from oven and cut into wedges. Makes 2 tortilla pies or 12 slices.

Never store tomatoes in the refrigerator. The cold temperature destroys the flavor and makes the flesh pulpy. Keep them at room temperature, but avoid direct sunlight. This will soften them without ripening.

MEXICAN FIESTA DIP

1   (16-ounce) can refried beans
1   package taco seasoning mix
2   large, ripe avocados
1   fresh lemon, squeezed for juice
    salt and pepper to taste
1   cup sour cream
2   large tomatoes, diced
1   small onion, diced small
1   (4 ½-ounce) can chopped, black olives
1½ cups grated, sharp Cheddar cheese
1½ cups grated Monterey Jack cheese
1   (4-ounce) can green chilies, chopped

In a large, glass serving bowl, start layering the following items as follows:
Layer 1—Mix refried beans with Taco mix and spread on bottom of bowl.
Layer 2—Mash avocados with lemon juice, salt and pepper; spread over beans.
Layer 3—Spread a layer of sour cream over these two.
Layer 4—Sprinkle tomatoes, onions and black olives next.
Layer 5—Sprinkle on mixed Cheddar and Monterey cheeses.
Layer 6—Decorate this layer with green chilies. Jalapenos may be used for more heat.

Chill in refrigerator at least 2 hours, to blend flavors. Serve with tortilla chips. Yield: 10-12 servings.

To seed an avocado; cut lengthwise around seed, then rotate both halves to separate. Insert knife firmly in seed, twist and lift out.

OYSTERS ON THE HALF SHELL

6-8　oysters per person
　　　crushed ice
　　　favorite cocktail sauce
　　　lettuce leaves for garnish (optional)
　　　lemon or lime wedges

Scrub oyster shells thoroughly, with a firm brush under cold, running water. Shuck oysters, leaving oysters on one shell, and removing any bits of shell around the shucked oyster. Arrange the oysters on a bed of crushed ice, placing lettuce around the edges, if desired. Place a smaller bowl of cocktail sauce in center of serving dish, and place enough lemon or lime wedges around for each person.

PINE ISLAND MARINATED SHRIMP

2　　pounds shrimp, steamed and peeled
½　　purple onion, sliced into rings
2　　tablespoons non-pareil capers
½　　cup canola oil
⅓　　cup vinegar
2　　teaspoons Worcestershire sauce
½　　tablespoon tabasco sauce
1　　teaspoon sugar
1　　teaspoon salt
⅛　　teaspoon pepper
　　　fresh parsley, chopped

Place shrimp, onion rings and capers in large shallow bowl. Combine canola oil, vinegar, Worcestershire, tabasco, sugar, salt and pepper in a measuring cup. Mix and pour over shrimp. Refrigerate for 24 hours, stirring occasionally.

Remove to a serving dish with a slotted spoon. Cover the shrimp with onion rings and capers. Garnish with parsley and serve. Yield: 10 servings.

SPICY STEAMED SHRIMP

¼   cup Old Bay seasoning
     water and beer
2   pounds fresh shrimp in the shell

In a steamer pot with a raised rack, fill equal amounts of water and beer to just below the level of the steamer rack. Layer shrimp, sprinkling the seasoning as you layer. Cover and steam approximately 3-4 minutes, or until shrimp are bright orange and fully cooked. Peel and eat! Serves 4. Shrimp are a low-calorie bargain-there are only 100 calories in a 3-ounce serving.

SPINACH DIP IN BREAD LOAF

2   cups sour cream (can use lite)
2   cups mayonnaise (can use lite)
1   package Knorr Vegetable Soup mix
1   package frozen, chopped spinach, thawed and
        drained
1   loaf sour dough bread
     fresh parsley, chopped

In a large bowl, mix sour cream, mayonnaise, soup mix and spinach until well blended. Remove the center of the sour dough loaf, scooping out the inside and leaving a well. Turn spinach dip into bread loaf and garnish with chopped parsley. Yield: a large appetizer to feed a crowd.

Shrimp are a low-calorie bargain–there are only 100 calories in a 3-ounce serving.

STEAMED CLAMS

6-12 clams per person (depending upon size)
salted water
melted butter
favorite cocktail sauce

Scrub shells well, under cold, running water to remove sand. Put clams in steamer with about 1 cup of water and 1 teaspoon of salt. Steam clams until they open, about 5-8 minutes. Discard any that do not open. Serve in the shell with melted butter and cocktail sauce.

TASTY TUNA DIP

1   cup grilled tuna bits (or leftover steaks)
1   package dry Italian salad dressing mix
1   cup sour cream

Combine all ingredients, stirring until blended; chill at least 4 hours. Serve with corn chips or melba rounds. Salmon, dolphin and other game fish substitute well. Yield: 1 ½ cups.

TOPSAIL BEACH SALSA

4   cups finely chopped fresh tomatoes
¼   cup finely diced green bell pepper
½   cup finely diced onion
¼   cup finely diced red bell pepper
½   cup cilantro leaves
4   jalapeno chiles, minced
1   tablespoon olive oil
1   tablespoon white vinegar
1   teaspoon salt
½   teaspoon minced garlic

Combine all ingredients in a medium bowl. Serve with tortilla chips. Makes 5 cups.

VIRGINIA DARE SHRIMP DIP

1   (8-ounce) package cream cheese, softened
1   (5-ounce) can small shrimp, mashed
2   tablespoons mayonnaise
2   tablespoons chili sauce
1   tablespoon lemon juice
¼   teaspoon curry powder
     chopped parsley for garnish

In a medium bowl, blend all ingredients thoroughly. Refrigerate at least 2 hours before serving, for flavors to blend. Just before serving, garnish with chopped parsley. Serve with crackers or chips. Yield: about 2 cups.

CARIBBEAN PUNCH

3   cups water
1   cup sugar
1   (12- ounce) can frozen orange juice concentrate, thawed
1   (6-ounce) can frozen lemonade concentrate, thawed
½   cup pineapple juice
3   medium-size, ripe bananas, mashed
2   cups light-colored rum (optional)
3   (12-ounce) cans ginger ale

Combine water and sugar in a saucepan; bring to a boil, stirring until sugar dissolves. Set sugar mixture aside.

Combine orange juice concentrate, lemonade concentrate, pineapple juice and mashed banana in blender container; process until smooth, stopping once to scrape down sides.

Combine sugar mixture and orange juice mixture in a large container. Add rum, if desired, and ginger ale, stirring well.

Cover and freeze.

Remove from freezer and let stand at room temperature 30 minutes before serving. Yield: about 3 ½ quarts.

CRANAPPLE WINE

¾   cup water
¾   cup sugar
2   (4-inch) sticks cinnamon
1   teaspoon whole cloves
    pinch of salt
3¼ cups Burgundy, chilled
3   cups cranapple juice, chilled

Combine water, sugar, cinnamon, whole cloves and salt in a saucepan. Bring to a boil, and remove from heat. Chill 8 hours. Strain and discard cinnamon and cloves. Combine syrup mixture, Burgundy, and cranapple juice. Yield: 7 ½ cups.

JACK DANIEL'S OUTER BANKS TEA

1   part Jack Daniels
½   part amaretto
3   parts pineapple juice
    splash of Coke
    Add ice!

When a slice of lemon is called for and the rest of the lemon not needed, slice it and freeze it in a plastic freezer bag. Lemon slices can then be used individually in ice water or other beverages for a refreshing treat.

ORANGE-LIME MARGARITAS

2   (6-ounce) cans frozen limeade concentrate, thawed
       and divided
1¼   cups tequila, divided
1   cup orange juice, divided
½   cup orange liqueur, divided
3   tablespoons powdered sugar, divided
       coarse salt
       lime wedges
       Garnish: lime slices

Process half of limeade concentrate, tequila, orange juice, orange liqueur and powdered sugar in a blender 30 seconds or until smooth. Add ice to bring to 3 ½-cup level; process until slushy. Pour into a large heavy-duty zip-top plastic bag; repeat procedure, and add to bag. Seal and freeze 8 hours.

Place salt in saucer. Rub rims of glasses with lime wedges; dip in salt.

Let margaritas stand at room temperature 20 minutes or until slushy; pour into glasses. Garnish, if desired. Yield: 6 cups.

PASSION FRUIT ICED TEA

6   orange pekoe tea bags
6   cups cold water
1   cup cranberry juice cocktail
⅔   cup passion-fruit juice concentrate, thawed
¼   cup honey

Put tea bags in a heatproof pitcher. In a saucepan, bring water just to a boil, and pour over the tea bags. Steep tea covered, three minutes and discard tea bags. Chill tea covered, until cold. Stir in the cranberry juice cocktail, passion-fruit concentrate and honey, stirring until combined well. Makes about 7 cups.

SANGRIA

½ gallon dry red wine
½ cup brandy
⅓ cup orange juice
2 tablespoons grated lemon rind
3 tablespoons fresh lemon juice
¾ cup sugar
1 apple, cored and cut into wedges
1 orange, sliced

Combine all ingredients, stirring until sugar dissolves; cover and chill at least 8 hours. Yield: 5 quarts.

SPARKLING GIN COOLER

3 cups orange juice, chilled
¾ cup gin
1 cup ginger ale, chilled
Garnishes: lime slices, maraschino cherries

Combine orange juice and gin. Add ginger ale, and stir gently. Pour over ice cubes, and garnish each glass with a lime slice and a maraschino cherry. Yield: about 5 cups.

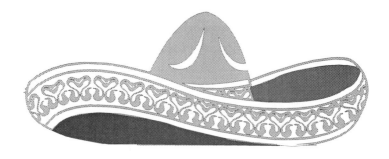

STRAWBERRY BANANA SMOOTHIE

½   banana, frozen
3   frozen strawberries, de-hulled
1   cup milk
1   tablespoon honey
2   ice cubes

Process all ingredients in a blender until smooth. Yield: 1 ½ cups.

WATERMELON LEMONADE

1   cup sugar
¼   cup water
2   cups peeled, seeded and diced watermelon
1   cup fresh lemon juice
1   quart carbonated water

Bring sugar and ¼ cup water to a boil over medium-high heat, stirring constantly, until sugar dissolves.

Press watermelon with back of a spoon through a fine wire-mesh strainer, discarding pulp. Combine watermelon juice, sugar syrup, and lemon juice in a 2-quart pitcher. Chill.

Add carbonated water to juice mixture just before serving; serve over ice. Yield: 2 quarts.

Breads

Breads

BAKED APPLE PANCAKE

3   tablespoon butter
2   golden delicious apples, peeled and chopped
     (about 2 cups)
¼   cup water
2   tablespoons sugar
½   teaspoon ground cinnamon
1   cup pancake mix plus the milk, oil and egg called
     for in package directions
½   cup shredded Cheddar cheese

Preheat oven to 350 degrees. Melt butter in non-stick 10-inch cast-iron skillet with ovenproof handle over medium heat (If handle is not oven-proof, wrap well in aluminum foil.) Stir in apple, water, 1 tablespoon sugar and cinnamon. Reduce heat to medium-low; cook until liquid evaporates and apples are tender, about 10 minutes. Remove skillet from heat.

While apples are cooking, prepare pancake batter according to package directions, adding the specified amounts of milk, oil and egg. Stir in shred-ded Cheddar and the remaining 1 tablespoon sugar just until blended. Spoon pancake batter evenly over apples in the skillet.

Bake pancake in preheated oven until set and springy when touched (about 10 or 12 minutes). Carefully remove skillet from oven and place on trivet. Cut the pancake into 8 wedges to serve. Serves 8.

BASIC CHEESE PIZZA

	yellow cornmeal for pizza pan
1	prepared or purchased pizza pie crust
1	cup chunky tomato sauce or bottled pizza sauce
¼	pound part-skim mozzarella cheese, shredded
3	tablespoons grated Parmesan cheese
1	teaspoon oregano

Preheat oven to 500 degrees. Sprinkle 12-inch pizza pan with a little cornmeal. Place pie crust in pan. Bake crust on lowest oven rack in preheated oven for 5 minutes or until lightly browned and crisp. Spread sauce evenly over pre-baked crust, leaving ½ inch border all around. Sprinkle mozzarella over sauce, followed by Parmesan and oregano. Bake in preheated oven for 8-10 minutes or until heated through, the cheese is melted and edge of crust is browned. Let stand for 5 minutes before cutting.

COMPANION RECIPE
CHUNKY TOMATO SAUCE

1	teaspoon olive oil
1	small onion, chopped
2	cloves garlic, finely chopped
1	can (28 ounces) Italian-style plum tomatoes, coarsely chopped
½	teaspoon salt
¼	teaspoon pepper

Lightly coat large non-stick skillet with olive oil. Heat over medium heat. Add onion; saute until softened, 5 minutes. Add garlic; saute 1 minute. Add tomatoes with their juice. Cook over medium heat, stirring occasionally, until thickened, about 30 minutes. Stir in salt and pepper. Use sauce immediately, or cool and then refrigerate, covered, for up to 4 days, or freeze for up to 1 month.

NOTE: It is often worthwhile to try to purchase pizza dough from any pizza place. They are more than happy to sell it to you, and your pizza will be so wonderful.

CORNCAKES

1   package (8½ ounce) corn muffin mix
1   cup corn kernels, drained
⅔   cup milk
1   large egg

In a medium bowl, mix all ingredients with a fork until blended, letting some lumps remain.

Coat a large non-stick skillet with non-stick spray; heat over medium-low heat. For each corncake, drop a scant ¼ cup batter onto skillet. Cook until golden brown on each side, spraying skillet between batches. Makes 10 - 12 corncakes.

EAST CAROLINA CORN BREAD

1   cup self-rising corn meal
1   small can cream-style corn
2   eggs
1   cup sour cream
1   teaspoon salt
2   teaspoons sugar

Mix together first three ingredients. Fold in sour cream, salt and sugar. Pour into an 8 x 8 inch greased pan. Bake at 350 degrees 20 to 25 minutes until done.

Small amounts of corn may be added to pancake batter for variety and flavor.

ELIZABETHAN TEA SCONES

2 cups all-purpose flour
2 tablespoons sugar
1 tablespoon baking powder
½ teaspoon salt
⅓ cup raisins
6 tablespoons butter or margarine
1 egg, beaten
½ cup milk
1 slightly beaten egg for brushing

Stir together flour, sugar, baking powder and salt in a medium size bowl. Add the raisins. Cut in the butter, until mixture resembles coarse crumbs. Add one beaten egg and milk, mixing until the dough clings together. Turn dough out on a lightly floured surface and gently knead about 12 strokes. Cut dough in half. Roll each half until it is ½ inch in thickness. Using a sharp knife, cut the dough into 8 wedges. Place the scones on ungreased baking sheet and brush with slightly beaten egg. Bake at 425 degrees, 12 minutes or until golden brown. Makes 12 to 15 scones.

FRISCO VEGETABLE WRAPS

2 tablespoons vegetable oil
1 medium red pepper, cut in 1" strips
2 medium green peppers, cut in 1" strips
1 large onion, peeled and cut in eighths
2 medium zucchini, thinly sliced
3 medium cloves garlic, minced
2 teaspoons chili powder
2 medium tomatoes, chopped
8 10" flour tortillas, warmed
2½ cups shredded Monterey Jack cheese

In a large skillet or wok, heat 2 tablespoons vegetable oil over medium heat. Add peppers, onion, zucchini, garlic and chili powder; cook 5 minutes, or until vegetables are tender. Stir in tomato; heat through. Spread portions of vegetables over each tortilla, then sprinkle with cheese. Fold sides over filling; roll up to make a burrito-style wrap. Yield: 8 servings.

GRILLED BACON, CHEESE AND TOMATO SANDWICHES

8   French bread slices
¼   cup butter or margarine, softened
8   (1-ounce) Jarlsberg or Swiss cheese slices
3   plum tomatoes, thinly sliced
½   teaspoon dried basil
2   cooked bacon slices

Spread one side of bread slices with butter; turn 4 slices buttered side down, and top each with a cheese slice. Layer evenly with tomato, basil, bacon, and remaining cheese slices; top with remaining bread slices, buttered side up.

Place a large skillet over medium heat until hot; cook sandwiches, 2 at a time, until golden, turning once. Yield: 4 servings.

HARKER'S ISLAND HUSH PUPPIES

¼   cup self-rising flour
1   cup self-rising corn meal
1   small onion, chopped
1   bell pepper, chopped (optional)
1   (8 ounce) can cream-style corn
    buttermilk (enough for a thick & pasty dough)

Mix flour, cornmeal, onion, bell pepper and cream-style corn together in a medium bowl. Add enough buttermilk to form a thick and pasty dough. Drop teaspoons full of dough into 350 degree cooking oil. This quantity of dough will make up to 20.

ISLAND-STYLE BANANA BREAD

2   cups all-purpose flour
1   teaspoon baking powder
½   teaspoon baking soda
¼   teaspoon salt
1½   teaspoons ground cinnamon
½   cup butter, softened
¾   cup packed brown sugar
2   slightly beaten eggs
1   teaspoon vanilla
1   cup mashed ripe bananas (about 3)
½   cup chopped pecans
1   (8-ounce) package reduced-fat cream cheese
1   egg
½   cup coconut

Preheat oven to 350 degrees. Grease bottom and ½-inch up sides of two 7½x3½x2-inch loaf pans; set aside. Combine flour, baking powder, baking soda, salt, and cinnamon; set aside. In a large bowl, beat butter with an electric mixer on high speed for 30 seconds. Add ½ cup of the brown sugar, the 2 eggs, and vanilla; beat until combined. Add dry mixture and mashed banana alternately to beaten mixture, beating on low speed after each addition until combined. Stir in pecans. In a medium bowl, beat cream cheese, remaining egg, and remaining ¼ cup brown sugar on medium speed until almost smooth. Stir in coconut.

Pour one-fourth of the banana batter into each loaf pan. Spoon one-fourth of the cheese mixture over each loaf. Using a spatula, cut through the batter to marble. Repeat the two layers as above, but do not marble. Bake about 50 minutes or until a toothpick inserted in center comes out clean. Cool in pans on wire rack for 10 minutes. Remove loaves from pans. Cool completely. Makes 2 loaves.

PAMLICO PEPPERY CHEESE BREAD

2½ cups all-purpose flour
1 tablespoon sugar
2 teaspoons cracked black pepper
1 teaspoon baking powder
¾ teaspoon salt
½ teaspoon baking soda
2 beaten eggs
1 carton (8 ounce) plain, low-fat yogurt
½ cup cooking oil
¼ cup milk
1 tablespoon spicy, brown mustard
1 cup shredded Cheddar cheese (4 ounce)
¼ cup thinly sliced green onion

Preheat oven to 350 degrees. Grease the bottom and ½ inch up the sides of an 8x4x2-inch loaf pan; set aside. In a large bowl stir together flour, sugar, pepper, baking powder, salt and soda. Make a well in center of dry mixture; set aside.

In a medium bowl combine eggs, yogurt, oil, milk and mustard. Add to dry mixture along with cheese and green onion. Stir just until moistened. Pour batter into prepared pan and spread evenly. Bake for 45 to 50 minutes or until a wooden toothpick inserted near center comes out clean. Cool on a wire rack for 10 minutes. Remove bread from pan. Cool for 1 hour on rack; serve warm. Makes 1 loaf.

Kneading the dough for a half minute after mixing improves the texture of baking powder biscuits.

QUICK GARLIC BREAD

1   (16-ounce) loaf unsliced French bread
½   cup butter, softened
1   tablespoon salad dressing
2   tablespoons grated Parmesan cheese
¼   teaspoon garlic powder
¼   teaspoon paprika

Cut French bread in half lengthwise. Combine butter and remaining ingredients; spread on cut sides of bread. Broil 4 inches from heat 4 to 5 minutes. Yield: 1 loaf.

RANCH-STYLE TORTILLA WRAPS

8   ounces reduced-fat cream cheese
1   cup light Ranch dressing
4   10-inch flour tortillas, warmed
10 ounces turkey breast slices
10 ounces Monterey Jack cheese slices
2   large avocados, peeled and thinly sliced
2   medium tomatoes, thinly sliced
    alfalfa sprouts

Blend together cream cheese and Ranch dressing. Spread evenly on warmed tortillas. Evenly layer turkey, cheese, avocados, tomatoes and sprouts, leaving a 1-inch border around the edges. Fold the bottom edge toward the center and firmly roll away from you until completely wrapped. Place seam side down and cut in half diagonally. Serves 4.

ROAST BEEF PITAS

¼	cup mayonnaise
2	tablespoons prepared horseradish
2	tablespoons sour cream
4	(6-inch) pita breads, cut crosswise
1	pound cooked roast beef, thinly sliced
16	slices tomato
	lettuce leaves, washed and crisped

In a small bowl, blend mayonnaise with horseradish and sour cream. Spread mixture in pita halves, dividing evenly. Arrange roast beef, lettuce and tomato slices in each pita. Yield: 8 servings.

SANDERLING SWEET POTATO BISCUITS

1	cup flour
3	teaspoons baking powder
½	teaspoon salt
4	tablespoons shortening
1	cup cooked, mashed sweet potatoes
½	cup milk

Sift flour, baking powder and salt together. Cut in shortening. Add sweet potatoes. Add milk gradually (adjust amount of milk slightly if necessary). Dough should be firm, but not stiff. Roll out on a floured surface. Cut with biscuit cutter. Place on greased baking sheet and bake at 400 degrees for 15 minutes or until lightly browned. Yield: 8-10 biscuits.

SNEAD'S FERRY 7-UP BISCUITS

2 cups all-purpose flour
4 teaspoons baking powder
½ teaspoon salt
½ cup shortening
¾ cup 7-Up

In a medium bowl, sift the dry ingredients together. Cut shortening in with a pastry blender. Add cold 7-Up and stir to form a soft ball. Turn onto a floured surface and knead the dough several times. Roll dough to ½" thickness and cut with a floured biscuit cutter. Place biscuits on an ungreased baking sheet and baste tops with melted butter. Bake at 450 degrees for 10-12 minutes.Yield: 12 biscuits.

SOUR CREAM MUFFINS

½ cup butter, softened
1 (8-ounce) carton sour cream
2 cup biscuit mix

Cream butter; stir in sour cream. Gradually add biscuit mix, stirring just until dry ingredients are moistened. Spoon into lightly greased miniature muffin pans, filling two-thirds full. Bake at 350 degrees for 15 minutes or until lightly browned. Yield: 3 dozen
NOTE: Muffins can be made in regular muffin pans. Bake at 350 degrees for 20 minutes. Yield: 1 dozen.

Soups & Salads

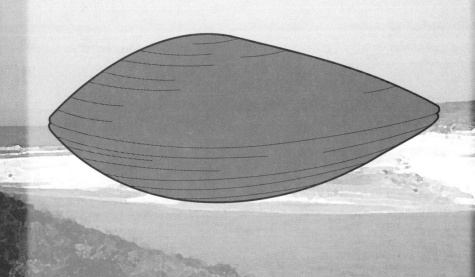

Soups & Salads

ATLANTIC BEACH BLACK BEAN SOUP

1	cup dried, black beans, cooked to package directions
	Or:
	3 cans prepared beans can be substituted
2	tablespoons olive oil
½	cup carrots, chopped
1	medium size onion, chopped
½	cup celery, chopped
1	clove garlic, crushed
1	can (10-ounce) tomatoes with green chilies
	salt and pepper to taste
¼	cup dry sherry
¼	cup minced cilantro
	lime slices for garnish (optional)

Soak beans overnight (if using dried), and cook according to package directions.

Heat olive oil in a large Dutch oven. Saute carrots, onion and celery 5 minutes or until tender. Add garlic and saute 1 or 2 minutes more. Add tomatoes, prepared beans, salt and pepper to taste. Heat to boiling; reduce heat and simmer 20 minutes. Cool; in a food processor puree half of the soup mixture. Return to pot and reheat. Just before serving, add sherry and cilantro. Stir gently and serve. May be served with lime slices if desired. Serves 6.

To chop an onion; cut peeled onion in half from stem to root end. Make horizontal cuts, then vertical cuts almost to root end. Slice across cuts, starting at stem end.

BOUILLABAISSE FROM THE VILLAGE OF DUCK

1   pound red snapper
1   pound catfish fillets
2   medium lobsters
¼   cup olive oil
1   cup sliced leeks
1   cup sliced onions
4   cloves garlic, minced
1   can (28 ounces) plum tomatoes, crushed
1   bay leaf
¼   teaspoon saffron strands
½   teaspoon dried thyme
½   teaspoon hot pepper sauce
2   teaspoons salt
¼   teaspoon black pepper
½   cup dry white wine
12   large clams, scrubbed well
1   pound large shrimp, peeled and deveined
6   slices French bread, buttered and toasted
    fresh chopped parsley

Have fish well cleaned, cut into slices 2 inches thick. Insert sharp knife between body and tail of lobster to sever spinal cord. Cut through shell and all into fairly large serving pieces; set aside.

Pour oil into large Dutch oven over medium-high heat; when hot, saute leeks and onions 2 minutes. Add garlic and saute another minute more. Add tomatoes, bay leaf, saffron, thyme, pepper sauce, salt and pepper. Stir gently and simmer over low heat 20-30 minutes.

Place lobster pieces into sauce, add fish, making sure all seafood is covered with liquid. Boil gently for about 8 minutes. Pour in wine, add clams and shrimp, cooking another 5-8 minutes, or until all shells are open. (Discard any that do not.)

Place French bread into shallow bowls; spoon seafood onto toast, cover with broth, sprinkle with parsley and serve piping hot. Serves 6.

BRUNSWICK STEW

1	(4-pound) stewing chicken, cut up
2	quarts water
2	teaspoons salt
½	cup catsup
2	teaspoons Worcestershire sauce
½	teaspoon hot pepper sauce
3	tablespoons butter or margarine
	grated rind and juice of ½ lemon
1	(28-32 ounce) can tomatoes, or 8 fresh
4	medium potatoes, diced
4	cups fresh baby lima beans
4	cups whole kernel corn
2	cups fresh okra, cut in ½ slices
4	stalks celery, cut in ½ slices
4	cloves garlic, minced
2	medium onions, diced
	salt and pepper to taste

Combine chicken, water and salt in Dutch oven. Simmer, covered, until meat is tender and falls off the bone. Remove chicken pieces with a slotted spoon and cool. Remove skin, then meat from the bones. Cut meat into bite-size pieces. Set aside.

Skim the chicken stock and return chicken meat to the pot. Add the catsup, Worcestershire sauce, hot pepper sauce, margarine, lemon and tomatoes. Stir and bring to a boil. Add potatoes, lima beans, corn, okra, celery, garlic and onions; stir. Season with salt and pepper to taste. Cover and simmer, stirring occasionally, until mixture is thick, about 1 ½ to 2 hours. Yield: 8 servings.

BUXTON BAKED BEAN SOUP

2 teaspoons vegetable oil
3 medium, all-purpose potatoes, peeled and diced
1 cup celery, sliced thin
1 small onion, chopped
1 pound green cabbage, shredded (about 6 cups)
4 cups chicken broth
1 bay leaf
½ teaspoon pepper
1 can (16 ounce) pork and beans in tomato sauce

Heat oil in a 3-quart saucepan. Add potatoes, celery and onion. Saute 5 minutes or until onion is tender. Stir in cabbage, cover and cook over medium heat, stirring occasionally, until cabbage is crisp-tender. Add broth, bay leaf and pepper. Bring to a boil and reduce heat. Simmer 20 minutes or until potatoes and cabbage are tender. Remove bay leaf.

Stir in beans and cook 10 minutes longer for flavors to blend and beans to heat through. Yield: 4 servings.

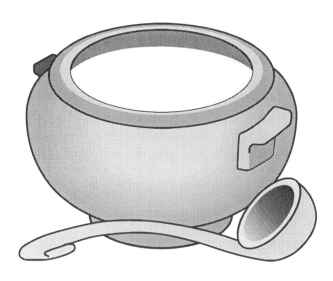

Soups and Salads

CAJUN CHICKEN AND CRAWFISH GUMBO

3	quarts water
1	frying chicken, cut up
½	cup vegetable oil
½	cup all-purpose flour
3	ribs celery, chopped fine
1	large onion, chopped fine
1	medium size green pepper, chopped fine
2	quarts reserved chicken stock
2	teaspoons salt
1	teaspoon black pepper
1	teaspoon cayenne (or blackened fish seasoning)
1	tablespoon chopped garlic
1	bunch green onions, chopped
1	bunch parsley, chopped
1	pound crawfish
3	cups hot, fluffy cooked rice

Heat water in a large Dutch oven over high heat. Add chicken when water boils, and cook on medium heat for 30 minutes. Remove from heat, and cool until chicken can be handled. Remove chicken from bones, reserving broth in a large bowl.

Heat the oil in the same pot until just below the stage of smoking. Carefully add the flour to the oil, whisking in a little at a time. Continue to whisk until the roux reaches the color of mahogany brown, approximately 10-12 minutes.

Add the celery, onions and green pepper to the roux and cook, stirring occasionally for 10 minutes. Add the chicken stock, chicken meat, salt, pepper, cayenne and garlic; bring to a rolling boil. Cook for 1 hour over medium heat.

Add the green onions, parsley and crawfish and cook for 10 minutes. Adjust seasoning if desired. Ladle 6-8 ounces of gumbo into large soup bowls. Top each bowl with ½ cup white rice. Serves 6.

CAPE FEAR CREAM OF CRAB SOUP

1	pound selected crab meat
1	chicken bouillon cube
1	cup boiling water
¼	cup chopped onion
¼	cup butter, melted
3	tablespoons flour
¼	teaspoon celery salt
1	teaspoon salt
	dash pepper
1	quart milk
	chopped parsley

Pick through the crab meat to remove any particles of shell. Dissolve bouillon cube in water. In a large saucepan, cook onion in butter until tender. Blend in flour and seasonings. Add milk and bouillon gradually; cook until thick, stirring constantly. Add crab meat; heat. Garnish with parsley. Serves 6.

CASWELL BEACH OYSTER STEW

1	quart fresh shucked oysters, in their liquid
4	tablespoons butter
2	stalks celery, diced
1	medium onion, diced
1	cup fresh mushrooms, sliced
¼	cup flour
1	cup white wine
1	cup reserved oyster liquid
2	teaspoons chicken bouillon granules
2	tablespoons fresh parsley, chopped
⅛	teaspoon thyme
⅛	teaspoon nutmeg
	desired amount of pepper
	fresh lemon juice to taste
1	cup heavy cream
2	tablespoons grated Parmesan cheese

Drain oysters, reserving liquid and set aside. Measure liquid and if necessary, add water to measure 1 cup; set aside.

In a saucepan, saute celery in butter, cooking on medium-low, about 2 minutes.

Add onions and mushrooms. Continue to cook until onions are clear. Stir in flour; add wine, oyster liquid and bouillon granules. Bring to a boil, stirring well.

Reduce heat, add seasonings, cream and cheese; blend well. Add oysters; cook until edges curl. (Do not overcook.) May be served with rice as a main entree or as a hearty stew. Yield: 6 servings.

CHILLED CARROT SOUP WITH GARDEN HERBS

6	tablespoons olive oil
5	large carrots, thinly sliced
2½	cups thinly sliced onions
1	teaspoon dried thyme
1	teaspoon brown sugar
½	teaspoon ground nutmeg
4	cups canned chicken broth
¼	cup orange juice
	salt and pepper to taste
	chopped fresh chives

Heat olive oil in a large saucepan over medium heat. Add carrots and onions and saute 4 minutes. Add thyme, brown sugar and nutmeg; saute until vegetables are tender, about 6 minutes. Add chicken broth. Cover pot; simmer until carrots are very soft, about 25 minutes. Using slotted spoon, transfer vegetables to processor. Add ¼ cup cooking liquid. Puree vegetables until smooth. Return puree to pot. Stir in orange juice. Season to taste with salt and pepper. Chill. Sprinkle with chives. Yield: 6 servings.

Add leftover cooked vegetables and cooked fish or seafood to prepared cream-based soup for a simple, super chowder.

CHOWAN COUNTY CHILE

2	pounds lean ground beef
1	large onion, chopped
1	green bell pepper, chopped
4	garlic cloves, minced
2½	cups water
1	(14 ½-ounce) can diced tomatoes, undrained
2	tablespoons chili powder
1	teaspoon salt
1	tablespoon dried oregano
1	tablespoon cocoa
1	tablespoon ground cumin
1½	teaspoons ground cinnamon
¾	teaspoon ground red pepper
2	beef bouillon cubes
1	(16-ounce) can kidney beans, undrained
	shredded Cheddar cheese
	chopped green onions

Cook beef in a large Dutch oven over medium heat, stirring until it crumbles and is no longer pink. Remove from Dutch oven, reserving juices and set aside.

Saute onion, bell pepper, and garlic in Dutch oven until tender. Add beef, water, tomatoes, spices, seasonings and bouillon cubes. Bring to a boil over medium heat, stirring often. Reduce heat; simmer, stirring occasionally, for 1 hour.

Stir in beans, and cook 5 minutes. Top each serving with cheese and green onions. Serve with cornbread or white rice, if desired. Yield: 6-8 servings.

CIOPPINO, CAROLINA STYLE

4	garlic cloves, minced
¼	cup olive oil
1	medium onion, chopped fine
½	teaspoon dried hot red pepper flakes
1	green bell pepper, chopped
1	tablespoon red-wine vinegar
1½	cups dry white wine
1	teaspoon dried oregano
1	bay leaf
1	can (28 ounce) whole tomatoes, pureed with juice
1	tablespoon tomato paste
6	soft-shelled crabs
12	large clams, scrubbed
½	pound medium shrimp, shelled
½	pound sea scallops
1	pound white fish fillet, (grouper, flounder, dolphin), cut into 1-inch pieces
2	tablespoon minced fresh parsley
3	cups cooked rice (or linguini)

In a heavy Dutch oven cook garlic and onion in oil over medium heat, stirring, until onion is softened and garlic is golden.

Add pepper flakes and bell pepper and cook, stirring, until softened. Add vinegar and boil until evaporated. Add wine, oregano and bay leaf and simmer 5 minutes. Stir in tomatoes and paste and bring to a boil. Simmer on low 15 minutes to blend flavors.

Add crabs, clams, shrimp, scallops and fish to soup. Simmer, covered for 5 minutes or until seafood is just cooked through, and clams open up. (Discard any unopened ones.) Sprinkle with fresh parsley and serve over rice or linguini. Serves 6.

Soups and Salads

CREAM OF (ANY VEGETABLE) SOUP

1½ pounds cauliflower, fresh spinach, broccoli, carrots, cabbage or potatoes, diced
1½ quarts water
½ stick butter
1 medium onion, diced
¼ cup celery, diced
4 tablespoons flour
4 cubes chicken bouillon
2 cups half-and-half
salt and pepper to taste

In a 2-quart saucepan, combine diced vegetable of choice with water. Simmer about 1/1/2 hours. Remove pan from heat.

In another large saucepan or stockpot, melt butter and saute onions and celery until transparent. Add flour and blend well.

Add vegetables (including cooking water) and bouillon cubes. Blend together until mixture thickens. Simmer for 5 minutes, stirring occasionally. Stir in half-and-half and salt and pepper to taste. Makes 8 servings.

To chop cabbage easily, hold the head steady on a work surface; cut in half with a chef's knife, through the stem end. With cabbage half flat-side up, cut out a wedged shaped core from stem end. Repeat with other half. Position cabbage half flat-side down; slice lengthwise into 1-inch strips. Rotate quarter-turn; cut crosswise.

CRESCENT BEACH CORN AND CRAB BISQUE

4	strips bacon
½	onion, finely chopped
½	cup celery, finely chopped
½	green pepper, finely chopped
½	red pepper, finely chopped
½	cup raw, peeled finely diced potatoes
3	cups water
¼	teaspoon paprika
1	bay leaf
3	tablespoons flour
2	cups milk, divided
2	cups cooked fresh corn
½	pound crab meat
	fresh parsley

Saute the bacon until crisp; remove and crumble. In the bacon drippings, saute onion, celery, and peppers until onion is soft, but not brown. Add the potatoes, water, bay leaf, paprika, and simmer until the potatoes are tender (35 to 40 minutes).

Reduce heat to the boiling point and add the flour and ½ cup of the milk. In a separate saucepan, heat crab meat, corn, and the remaining milk. When warmed through, add this and bacon to the soup mixture. Heat on low for a few minutes. Do not boil. Garnish with parsley and serve. Yield: 6 servings.

CROATAN 13-BEAN SOUP

4	cups dried 13-bean mix
¼	pound salt pork, country ham or smoked sausage
4	quarts water
1	medium size onion, chopped
2	cloves garlic, minced
1	can (28-ounce) crushed tomatoes
	hot pepper sauce to taste
½	cup dried parsley
2	tablespoons dried basil
1	teaspoon oregano
	salt and pepper to taste

Wash and rinse beans thoroughly. In a large Dutch oven, place beans, meat and water; simmer on medium-low heat 2 hours. Add vegetables, hot pepper sauce and seasonings. Simmer 1 hour more. Serve hot. Yield: 8-10 servings.

FISH STOCK

1	pound bones and trimmings from any white fish
2	tablespoons butter
1	onion, chopped
12	sprigs of fresh parsley
2	tablespoons fresh lemon juice
½	teaspoon salt
3	cups cold water
¾	cup dry white wine

Chop fish bones and trimmings. Heat a heavy saucepan over medium heat and melt butter. Add fish trimmings, onion, parsley, lemon juice and salt. Cook, covered, for 5 minutes. Add water and wine and bring to a boil, skimming froth. Simmer stock 20 minutes and pour through a fine sieve for further use. Fish stock may be frozen for up to three months. Yield: 3 cups.

FORT SUMTER FISH CHOWDER

3   slices bacon
¾   cup chopped onion
½   cup diced celery
½   cup diced carrots
2   cups diced potatoes
    water
1-2 pounds fish fillets (flounder, snapper, grouper other
    firm-meat fish)
1   teaspoon salt
⅛   teaspoon pepper
⅛   teaspoon thyme
⅛   teaspoon paprika
1   quart half-and-half
¼   cup sliced scallions

In a Dutch oven, saute bacon until crisp. Remove and save. Add onion and celery; cook over medium heat until tender, but not brown. Add carrots and potatoes, and cover with water. Simmer until vegetables are almost cooked, and add fish. Simmer until vegetables are tender, and fish flakes easily with a fork. Season with salt, pepper, thyme and paprika. Gradually add half-and-half, and heat, stirring constantly. Simmer (do not boil) for 10 minutes until seafood is done. Garnish with sliced scallion and crumbled bacon bits. Yield: 6 servings.

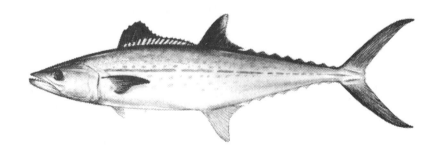

HATTERAS CLAM CHOWDER

¼	pound bacon
5	cups water
3	white potatoes, diced
2	onions, diced
3	stalks celery, diced
¼	teaspoon thyme
½	teaspoon salt
¼	teaspoon pepper
	parsley for garnish

Cook bacon crispy, reserving fat. Cool and crumble, set aside. Heat water in a large saucepan or Dutch oven, adding bacon drippings. Add potatoes and cook 5 minutes. Add onions and celery; cook an additional 10 minutes. Add clams, juice, bacon and seasonings. (Chop clams into small pieces, if using fresh.) Simmer for 15 to 20 minutes more, or until desired consistency. Do not overcook, for clams will toughen. Garnish with parsley. Yield: 6 servings.

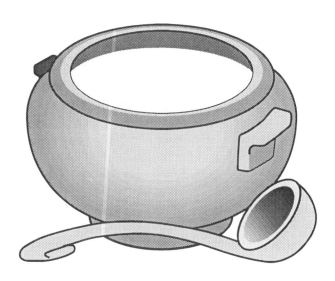

ISLAND CONCH CHOWDER

3	slices bacon
1	yellow onion, diced
2	carrots, peeled and sliced
1	(16 ounce) can tomatoes
2	potatoes, peeled and sliced
1	jalapeno pepper, sliced
1	tablespoon beef bouillon
1	pound conch meat, canned or fresh
2	tablespoons butter, melted
1	large can corn
4-5	cups water
	salt to taste
	sherry to garnish

In a Dutch oven, saute the bacon till crispy. Remove, leaving drippings in pan. Saute onion and carrots till onions are clear. Add the tomatoes, potatoes, pepper and bouillon. Simmer, covered until the potatoes are almost tender.

Warm a saute pan over medium heat. Melt the butter and saute the conch for about 1 minute. Add the conch to the tomato mixture. Stir in the corn, water and salt. Cook until it boils. Crumble crispy bacon on top and serve with the sherry bottle to add a great flavor. Serves 8.

To store seafood uncooked–refrigerate tightly covered in original package 1 to 2 days. Freeze in airtight container up to 4 months. Thaw in refrigerator. To store cooked fish–refrigerate tightly covered 1 to 2 days. Freeze tightly wrapped up to 2 months. Thaw in refrigerator.

Soups and Salads

PAMLICO SPLIT PEA SOUP

1½   cups finely minced onions (2 large onions)
¾   cup diced ham (¼ pound)
3   tablespoons vegetable oil
2   cups split peas, washed and rinsed
1   ham bone
12   cups hot tap water
½   cup chicken stock or bouillon
1½   teaspoons sugar
1¼   teaspoons salt
½   teaspoon black pepper
¼   teaspoon tabasco
1   cup diced potatoes
1   cup diced carrots

In a soup pot, saute the onions and ham in the vegetable oil, until the onions are translucent, about 2-3 minutes. Add the split peas, ham bone, water, and stock or bouillon. Cook the soup over medium to medium-high heat 50-60 minutes or until the soup is smooth. Add the sugar, salt, pepper and tabasco.

Add the potatoes and carrots for the last 25 minutes of cooking time. Serves 6.

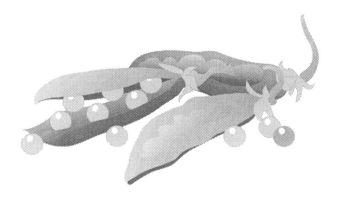

TORTILLA SOUP - MANZANILLA STYLE

½   cup onion, chopped
1   clove garlic, minced
1   tablespoon butter or margarine
4   cups chicken broth
1   whole chicken breast
1   (14-ounce) can tomatoes, cut up
1   (8-ounce) can tomato sauce
1   (3-ounce) can chili peppers, drained and cut
¼   cup cilantro or parsley, chopped
1   teaspoon oregano
6   corn tortillas
     canola oil
1   cup Monterey Jack cheese, shredded (4 ounces)
     sliced avocado, for garnish

In a 3-quart saucepan, cook onion and garlic in butter till tender and just clear. Stir in chicken broth, chicken breast, tomatoes, tomato sauce, chili peppers, cilantro or parsley, and oregano. Bring to a boil. Reduce heat and simmer, covered, for 35-40 minutes. Remove chicken breast to a plate to cool.

Meanwhile, cut tortillas in half, then cut crosswise into ½ -inch-wide strips. In a heavy skillet heat ½ inch of canola oil. Fry strips in hot oil, about half at a time, for 40-45 seconds or till crisp and light brown. Drain on paper towels.

When chicken is cool enough to handle, but still warm, shred chicken meat into the soup. Divide fried tortilla strips and cheese among soup bowls. Place soup bowls in a pre-heated 300 degree oven for a few minutes to melt the cheese. Remove bowls from oven, carefully, as they will be hot. Ladle soup over tortilla strips and cheese. Garnish with sliced avocado. Serve immediately. Makes 6 to 8 servings.

CALABASH COLE SLAW

1	small head cabbage
1	large apple
1	small can pineapple chunks
½	cup raisins
	desired amount mayonnaise
½	cup almonds or walnuts (optional)

Chop cabbage and wash well. Peel apple and chop into cabbage. Add pineapple and ½ of juice from can. Add raisins. Add mayonnaise to desired taste and consistency. Toss well, and store in covered container. Add optional nuts just before serving. Yield: 6 to 8 servings.

FOLLY BEACH GARLIC VINAIGRETTE

½	cup olive oil
¼	cup red wine vinegar
2	tablespoons fresh lemon juice
2	tablespoons water
1½	teaspoons minced garlic
½	teaspoon salt

Pour ingredients into blender jar. Process until well blended. Makes 1 cup.

HERB VINEGAR

1	small sprig thyme
1	small sprig rosemary
1	small bay leaf
1	pint white wine vinegar
1	large clove garlic
1	strip orange peel (1"x4")

Put the thyme, rosemary, bay leaf, garlic and orange peel into a 1-pint bottle. Add the wine vinegar and seal. Store for a month before using, giving the bottle a very gentle shake every day or two.

Use as a salad dressing, or a marinade for grilled or broiled meats or steamed vegetables. Or add a dash to your favorite soup to brighten the flavor.

JAMES ISLAND MARINATED SHRIMP AND PASTA SALAD

2	cups uncooked pasta shells
1	can (4 ½-ounce) medium shrimp
½	cup vegetable oil
½	cup lemon juice
1	package (.7-ounce) Italian salad dressing mix
1	teaspoon prepared horseradish
1½	cups small broccoli flowerettes
1	cup coarsely shredded carrots
1½	cups sliced zucchini .
¼	cup green onions, chopped
	lettuce leaves

Cook pasta shells according to package directions; rinse under cold water and set aside to cool, then refrigerate. Drain shrimp and place in a small bowl. Set aside.

In a small jar with tight-fitting lid or cruet, combine oil, lemon juice, salad dressing mix and horseradish; shake well. In a small bowl, pour mixture over shrimp and refrigerate to marinate for two hours. In large bowl, combine this marinated shrimp mixture with cooked pasta, broccoli, carrots, zucchini and green onions and toss to mix thoroughly. Chill several hours or overnight, stirring occasionally. Serve on fresh lettuce leaves. Makes 8-10 servings.

Soups and Salads

KNOTT'S ISLAND CHICKEN SALAD SUPREME

4   cups diced cooked chicken
¾   cup dark or golden raisins
¾   cup drained pineapple tidbits
1   teaspoon dijon mustard
1   teaspoon curry powder
¾   cup mayonnaise
⅓   cup chopped celery
     lettuce
½   cup chopped pecans

In a large bowl, blend together chicken, raisins, pineapple, mustard, curry powder, mayonnaise and celery.

Place four large servings on bed of lettuce. Top each serving with chopped pecans. Makes 6 servings.

LITCHFIELD BEACH BROCCOLI SALAD

3   broccoli crowns
½   cup mayonnaise
3   tablespoons sugar
2   tablespoons cider vinegar
½   cup onion, chopped
4   strips crisp bacon, crumbled
¼   cup raisins
¼   cup pecans, broken

Soak broccoli crowns in cold water 5 minutes. Drain well. Chop broccoli crowns and some of the stems. Set aside.

In a large bowl, mix mayonnaise, sugar and vinegar. Add broccoli, onion, bacon, and raisins. Toss gently to cover. Place in serving dish, and sprinkle with pecans. Yield: 6 servings.

MAGNOLIA PLANTATION HOT PEPPER VINEGAR

8-10 hot chili peppers (red or green or both)
    white vinegar
1   clove garlic, peeled (optional)

Put a small hole at end of each chili pepper and pack loosely into a vinegar cruet or similar container. Score garlic clove with a knife and add to the peppers. (Garlic is optional). Pour vinegar over the peppers and allow to stand for several days before using. Only the vinegar is used, the peppers remain in the container. More vinegar can be added as the original supply is used up. Replace the peppers when the sauce begins to lose its zip. Enjoy over your favorite vegetables - mine are collards!

MYRTLE BEACH STEAK SALAD WITH PEACH SALSA

1   (1-pound) flank steak
1   tablespoon dark sesame oil, divided
2   tablespoons fresh ginger, minced
1   clove garlic, minced
4   cups mixed salad greens
1   tablespoon lime juice
    peach salsa (recipe this book)

Place steak between 2 sheets of heavy-duty plastic wrap, and flatten to ⅛-inch thickness using a meat mallet or rolling pin; cut into ½-inch strips. Combine 2 teaspoons oil, ginger, and garlic; stir in beef. Roll strips into pinwheels. Secure with a toothpick.

Heat a skillet over high heat; add steak, and cook 1 minute on each side or until browned.

Toss salad greens with remaining 1 teaspoon oil and lime juice. Serve immediately with steak pinwheels and peach salsa. Serves 4.

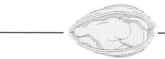

NEW BERN BALSAMIC VINAIGRETTE

¼   cup balsamic vinegar
1   tablespoon honey
1   teaspoon fresh thyme leaves
1   teaspoon dijon mustard
¼   teaspoon salt
¼   teaspoon freshly ground black pepper
¼   cup olive oil

In a blender, blend vinegar, honey, thyme leaves, Dijon mustard, salt and pepper. With motor running, add oil in a slow stream and blend until emulsified. Makes about ½ cup.

PINEY GREEN CURRIED CHICKEN SALAD

3   cups cooked chicken, cut into bite-size pieces
1   container plain yogurt
1   rib celery, sliced thin
¾   cup seedless grapes (red & green), cut in half
1   can (8 ounce) pineapple chunks, drained
⅓   cup mango chutney
2   teaspoons curry powder
6   cups assorted greens, washed, trimmed and crisped
½   cup chopped peanuts for garnish (optional)

Mix all ingredients except greens and peanuts in a medium bowl until blended. Serve over crisp greens. Garnish with chopped nuts, if desired. Serves 6.

PLEASURE ISLAND PEPPER RELISH

2 large green peppers, ground
2 large red peppers, ground
1 medium onion, ground
¼ cup sugar
1 teaspoon salt
1 teaspoon mustard seed
⅓ cup cider vinegar

Pour boiling water over ground peppers and onions to cover; cover with lid and let stand 20 minutes. Drain well. Add sugar, salt, mustard seed and vinegar; and simmer 15 minutes. Chill well before serving. Makes 2 cups relish.

RASPBERRY POPPY SEED DRESSING

½ cup sugar
½ teaspoon salt
1 teaspoon dry mustard
1 teaspoon grated onion
⅓ cup raspberry vinegar
1 cup canola oil
2 tablespoons poppy seeds

In a medium, bowl, mix together sugar, salt, mustard, onion and vinegar. Add oil by pouring in a thin stream, beating constantly until thickened. Add poppy seeds, and beat a few minutes more. Refrigerate. Shake before serving.

SALTER PATH PICNIC PASTA SALAD

1	(16-ounce) box of medium-size pasta shells
1	bunch broccoli, cut into bite-size pieces
1	cup reduced-fat mayonnaise
½	cup reduced-fat sour cream
¼	cup dijon-style mustard
2	tablespoons white wine vinegar
2	tablespoons sugar
1	teaspoon dried tarragon
1	teaspoon salt
½	teaspoon pepper
1	red pepper, chopped
1	medium onion, chopped
1	(6 ½-ounce) can of your favorite: chicken, tuna, lobster, crab or shrimp

Fill a large Dutch oven with water and bring to a boil. Add pasta and broccoli and cook over medium heat about 5 minutes, or until pasta and broccoli are almost cooked. (Pasta will be aldente and broccoli firm). Drain pasta and broccoli; rinse under cold water and drain again.

In a medium bowl, mix mayonnaise, sour cream, mustard, vinegar, sugar, and spices. In a large mixing bowl, toss pasta and broccoli, onions, pepper, chicken (or seafood), and mayonnaise mixture together, until well blended. Cover and refrigerate until serving. Yield: 12 servings.

SPICY SEAFOOD COCKTAIL SAUCE

⅓	cup chili sauce
2	tablespoons lemon juice
1	tablespoon prepared horseradish
1	teaspoon Worcestershire sauce
2	drops bottled hot pepper sauce

Combine ingredients and chill thoroughly. Serve over shrimp and other seafood, cold or hot. Makes about ½ cup.

SURFSIDE FRESH TUNA SALAD

2   cups cooked, flaked tuna
½   cup chopped onion
½   cup chopped celery
¼   cup pickle relish
1   hard boiled egg, chopped
½   cup mayonnaise
1   tablespoon lemon juice
1   teaspoon salt
½   cup chopped nuts (pecans, walnuts optional)

In a large bowl, combine fish, onion, celery, relish and egg. In a small bowl mix mayonnaise, juice and salt. Pour over fish combination and toss gently until well coated. Sprinkle with chopped nuts, if desired, and toss once more. Serves 4.

SWAN QUARTER SHRIMP SALAD

1   pound small to medium sized shrimp
½   cup mayonnaise
2   teaspoons Old Bay seasoning
2   teaspoons lemon juice
⅓   cup celery, chopped
     lettuce leaves

In a steamer pot, steam shrimp until they turn pink and the tails curl, (about 3 minutes from boiling). Set aside to cool enough to peel and clean. In a medium bowl, mix mayonnaise, seasoning and lemon juice until blended. Toss in cleaned, peeled shrimp and celery until coated. Serve on a bed of lettuce. Serves 4.

Soups and Salads

TARTAR SAUCE

1   cup mayonnaise
¼   teaspoon grated onion
1   tablespoon vinegar
⅓   cup sweet-pickle relish
1   tablespoon green olives, chopped
1   tablespoon capers, chopped
1   teaspoon chopped parsley
     salt to taste

Blend mayonnaise, grated onion and vinegar. Add pickle relish, green olives, capers and parsley. Blend well and season to taste. Yield: 1½ cups.

Vegetables & Casseroles

Vegetables & Casseroles

BALD HEAD ISLAND'S ROASTED GARLIC

3   garlic bulbs
1-2 tablespoons olive oil

Peel away the dry outer leaves of each garlic bulb. Slice about ¼" off the tops, so each clove is exposed. Place the garlic bulbs in a small, covered baking dish, cut side up. Drizzle the olive oil over the garlic and cover. (Foil may be used, or a clay garlic baker if handy). Bake the garlic in a 350 degrees oven for 45 minutes or until the garlic is soft. The garlic paste should press from each clove easily to be spread on crusty bread. One clove will serve 4.

BUTTERED ASPARAGUS SPEARS

3   pounds fresh asparagus
2   quarts water
¼   cup butter or margarine
½   teaspoon salt
½   teaspoon freshly ground pepper

Trim tough ends of asparagus. Bring 2 quarts of water to a boil in a Dutch oven; add asparagus, and cook 3 to 5 minutes or until crisp-tender. Drain and rinse with cold water.

Melt butter in a large skillet; add asparagus, salt, and pepper, and saute until thoroughly heated. Yield: 8 servings.

CARAMELIZED SWEET VIDALIA ONIONS

1 cup balsamic vinegar
2 large, sweet Vidalia onions, skinned and cut in half crosswise
2 tablespoons butter or margarine
1 cup walnut halves
¼ cup firmly packed brown sugar
¼ cup chopped sweet yellow pepper
¼ cup chopped sweet red pepper
¼ teaspoon ground red pepper
fresh pineapple for garnish

Bring vinegar to a boil in a cast-iron skillet over medium-high heat. Remove from heat; place onions, cut side down, in skillet. Bake at 400 degrees for 55 to 60 minutes or until onions are tender and vinegar turns the color of dark chocolate.

Melt butter in skillet over medium heat; add walnuts, and cook 2 minutes, stirring often. Add sugar, red and yellow peppers, and ground red pepper; cook, stirring often, until mixture is bubbly.

Place an onion half, cut side up, on each plate. Sprinkle walnut mixture evenly around onions; drizzle with vinegar. Garnish, if desired. Serve immediately. Yield: 4 servings.

CAT ISLAND NUTTY STUFFED MUSHROOMS

1¼	pound large fresh mushrooms
2	tablespoons olive oil
3	tablespoons butter
2	cloves garlic, minced
⅓	cup walnuts, chopped
⅔	cup herb stuffing
½	cup Parmesan cheese, grated
1	large egg, beaten
¼	teaspoon salt

Remove stems from mushrooms and chop. Brush mushroom caps with brush to clean. Brush insides with oil. Melt butter in a small skillet, add stems, garlic and walnuts. Saute 3 to 4 minutes.

Prepare stuffing according to package directions. Mix prepared stuffing, sauteed walnut and garlic mixture, cheese, egg, and salt together. Stuff mushroom caps and place on an ungreased baking sheet. Bake at 350 degrees for 13 to 15 minutes. Serves 6.

To clean mushrooms; wipe with a damp paper towel or soft brush. Rinse quickly only if very dirty.

CEDAR ISLAND CREAMED SPINACH

12 ounces fresh spinach
1 small shallot
1 small clove garlic
1 tablespoon water
1 tablespoon unsalted butter
1 tablespoon all-purpose flour
¾ cup half-and-half

Remove coarse stems from spinach and rinse in a colander. In a large saucepan, cook spinach with water still clinging to leaves, covered, over moderate heat, stirring occasionally, until wilted, about 2 minutes. Transfer spinach to paper towels and squeeze to remove any excess liquid. Finely chop shallot and garlic and in saucepan, cook with water, covered over moderate heat until softened. Add butter and melt, stirring; add flour and cook roux, stirring. Add half-and-half in a slow stream, whisking, and simmer, whisking constantly, for 5 minutes. Stir in spinach and season with salt and pepper. Cook creamed spinach until heated through. Serves 2.

CORN GRILLED-IN-THE-HUSK

4-6 ears of corn, husks on
oil for brushing
salt and butter for flavor (optional)

Soak the corn cobs in hand-hot water for 20 minutes. Drain them thoroughly. Tear off all but the last two layers of outer leaves and brush with oil. Cook over a hot barbecue for 40 minutes, brushing with oil once or twice, and turning occasionally. Serve hot, adding a small amount of butter and salt if you desire. Serves 6-8.

Vegetables & Casseroles

CORNBREAD-STUFFED TOMATOES

1   (6-ounce) package cornbread mix
6   firm, ripe tomatoes
6   bacon slices, cooked and crumbled
4   green onions, chopped
¼   cup mayonnaise
¼   teaspoon salt
¼   teaspoon pepper
¼   cup grated Parmesan cheese

Cook cornbread according to package directions; cool and crumble into a bowl. Cut a ¼-inch slice from each tomato: scoop pulp into bowl with cornbread, leaving tomato shells intact. Place shells, upside down, on a paper towel to drain.

Stir crumbled bacon, green onions, mayonnaise, salt and pepper into cornbread mixture. Spoon mixture into tomato shells, and place in an 11x7-inch baking dish. Sprinkle with grated Parmesan cheese. Bake at 375 degrees for 15 minutes or until filling is thoroughly heated. Yield: 6 servings.

DILLY BEANS

1   pounds green beans, trimmed
1   teaspoon cayenne pepper
4   cloves garlic
4   heads dill
2½   cups water
2½   cups vinegar
¼   cup salt

Pack beans into hot jars, leaving ¼-inch head space. Add ¼ teaspoon pepper, 1 clove garlic and 1 head dill to each pint. Combine remaining ingredients in saucepan; bring to a boil. Pour boiling hot mixture over beans, leaving ¼-inch head space. Adjust caps. Process for 10 minutes in boiling water bath. Let beans stand for 2 to 4 weeks to allow the flavors to blend. Yield: 4 pints.

FRIED GREEN TOMATOES

4   medium green tomatoes
1   cup cornmeal
½   cup flour
1   tablespoon sugar
     salt and pepper to taste
     vegetable or canola oil for frying

Wash and slice tomatoes ½-inch thick. Mix cornmeal, flour and seasonings in a small bowl. Batter each tomato slice, being sure to coat both sides. Heat ¼-inch oil in a heavy skillet over medium heat. Fry tomatoes , about 2 minutes each side, until golden brown. Remove and drain on paper towels. Serves 4.

FRIPP ISLAND FRIED ONION RINGS

½   cup cornmeal
½   cup flour
     salt and pepper
1   egg, well beaten
½   cup milk
2   tablespoons butter or margarine, melted
2   medium size yellow onions
     vegetable oil for frying

In a medium bowl, add cornmeal, flour, salt and pepper to taste, egg and milk. Stir and blend thoroughly. Stir in melted butter.

Peel the onions and slice into ¼-inch crosswise slices. Separate the rings. Heat the vegetable oil to 375 degrees. Dip the onion rings in the batter, making sure they are thoroughly coated. Fry in hot vegetable oil about 2 minutes until delicately browned. Drain on paper towels. Serves 6-8.

GARDEN FRESH COLLARDS WITH GARLIC & OIL

8   cups fresh collards, washed and sliced
1   teaspoon salt
    water for steaming
2   teaspoons sugar
    pinch baking soda
2   tablespoons olive oil, divided
2   large cloves garlic, minced

Bring water level to bottom of steamer in a steaming pot. Bring to a boil over high heat. Add collards and salt. Cover and reduce heat to medium. Steam collards until not quite tender (7 to 8 minutes). Add sugar over the top of collards, and the baking soda to the steaming water by lifting the steamer. The boiling water will bubble up, giving the collards a brilliant green color. Steam an additional 2 to 3 minutes until collards are tender, but not mushy. Remove from heat and drain the water.

In a large saute pan, heat 1 tablespoon of oil and saute garlic until lightly browned. Remove the saute pan from the heat and toss in the steamed collards. Turn the collards to coat with oil and garlic. The additional table-spoon of oil may be added, if desired, by drizzling slowly while turning the collards in the pan. Turn out onto a serving dish and serve immediately. Serves 4.

The advantages of steaming vegetables far outweigh other cooking methods. It is quick, helps retain nutritional content of vegetables and prevents them from getting soft and mushy as some can when boiled. The collapsible metal steamer basket is a must for this method, as it will fit into most any pot.

GARLIC MASHED POTATOES FROM COLINGTON

3   cups mashed potatoes
1   cup sour cream
¼   cup milk
¼   teaspoon minced garlic
1   can french fried onions
1   cup shredded Cheddar cheese
⅓   cup chopped chives

Combine mashed potatoes, sour cream, milk and garlic in a large bowl. Spoon half the mixture into a 2-quart casserole sprayed with vegetable spray. Sprinkle with half of the onions and cheese. Top with remaining potato mixture. Bake 30 minutes in a 350 degrees oven. Top with remaining onions and cheese. Bake 5 minutes more until onions are golden and cheese is melted. Garnish with chopped chives. Serves 6.

GOOSE CREEK TOMATO-ZUCCHINI GRATIN

3   medium zucchini, thinly sliced
4   medium-size ripe tomatoes, peeled and thinly sliced
¾   cup grated Parmesan cheese, divided
2   cloves garlic, minced
1   teaspoon dried thyme
¼   teaspoon salt
¼   teaspoon pepper
2   tablespoons olive oil

Arrange half of zucchini slices in bottom of an ungreased 8-inch square baking dish; top with half of tomato slices. Sprinkle with ¼ cup Parmesan cheese.

Top with remaining zucchini and tomatoes. Sprinkle garlic, thyme, salt, and pepper over tomatoes; drizzle with olive oil. Sprinkle remaining Parmesan cheese over top.

Bake at 400 degrees for 20 to 25 minutes. Serve with a slotted spoon. Yield: 6 servings.

GRILLED VEGETABLES WITH HERB DRESSING

2	garlic cloves, crushed
2	tablespoons olive oil
1	red bell pepper, cored, seeded and cut into quarters
1	small zucchini, cut lengthwise and widthwise
1	large portobello mushroom, quartered
1	green onion, trimmed
2	small new potatoes, cooked and halved
	salt and freshly ground black pepper

Herb dressing:

1	teaspoon minced fresh savory
$\frac{1}{4}$	teaspoon crushed, dried thyme
$\frac{1}{4}$	teaspoon freshly ground black pepper
	salt
1	tablespoon olive oil
1	tablespoon balsamic vinegar

Combine garlic and olive oil in a cup and set aside 30 minutes. Brush pepper, zucchini, mushroom, green onion and potatoes with garlic oil. Place vegetables in a grilling basket and grill over medium-high heat for about 15 minutes or until done. (Some vegetables may cook quicker than others depending on their thickness; remove these first.)

While vegetables are grilling, combine savory, thyme, pepper, salt, olive oil and balsamic vinegar. Stir well to blend.

Place cooked vegetables in a bowl. Pour Herb Dressing over top and toss gently. Season with salt and pepper. Serve at room temperature. Yield: 2 servings. (Recipe may be doubled and tripled to yield more servings.)

While you've got the grill going this summer, use it to prepare dessert. Wash, dry, and core cooking apples. Fill centers with brown sugar and butter, wrap each apple in foil, and place in small foil pie tins on the grill. When the apples are tender, unwrap them and serve.

LITTLE RIVER TWICE-BAKED POTATOES

4   (8-ounce) russet potatoes, scrubbed
¾   cup cottage cheese
¼   cup sliced green onions
2   tablespoons milk
2   tablespoons butter
¼   teaspoon salt
⅛   teaspoon pepper
   bacon bits for garnish (optional)
¼   cup shredded Cheddar cheese

Heat oven to 400 degrees. Arrange potatoes directly on oven rack and bake 45 to 50 minutes until tender when pierced with a fork. When cool enough to handle, split open tops and, working over a medium-size bowl, scoop out potatoes, leaving ¼" thick shells. Add cottage cheese, green onions, milk, butter, salt and pepper to bowl and mash until blended and smooth. Spoon mixture into shells; sprinkle tops with cheese. Arrange in a shallow baking pan. Return to oven and bake about 15 minutes until filling is hot and cheese is melted. Sprinkle with bacon bits and serve. Makes 4 potatoes.

NEW HANOVER HERB-ROASTED POTATOES

⅓   cup dijon mustard
2   tablespoons olive oil
1   clove garlic, chopped
½   teaspoon Italian seasoning
6   medium red-skinned potatoes cut in chunks
   (about 2 pounds)

Mix mustard, olive oil, garlic and Italian seasoning in a small bowl. Place potatoes on lightly greased 13x9x2-inch baking pan or on shallow baking sheet; brush with mustard mixture. Bake at 425 degrees for 35 to 40 minutes or until potatoes are fork tender, stirring occasionally. Makes 4 servings.

PARMESAN-ZUCCHINI FRIES

1   cup fine, dry breadcrumbs
1   cup grated Parmesan cheese
½   teaspoon salt
2   medium zucchini
2   large eggs, lightly beaten
     vegetable oil

Combine breadcrumbs, cheese and salt; set aside. Cut zucchini into thin strips; dip into egg, and dredge in breadcrumb mixture.

Pour oil to depth of 2 inches into a Dutch oven or heavy saucepan; heat to 375 degrees. Fry zucchini in oil until golden brown. Drain on paper towels. Serve immediately. Yield: 4 to 6 servings.

POBLANO PEPPERS STUFFED WITH SHRIMP

4   Poblano peppers
2   cups cooked (and cooled) rice
2   teaspoons butter or margarine
½   cup chopped onion
1   cup small fresh shrimp, cleaned
¼   cup Parmesan cheese
½   cup French dressing, diluted with -
1   tablespoon white wine
½   teaspoon salt
2   tablespoons chopped parsley
     desired amount of freshly ground pepper

Slice tops off peppers, and remove seeds. Steam peppers for about 2 minutes, run under cold water and drain. Peppers should be partially cooked, but still firm. In a medium pan, sautee onions and fresh shrimp in the butter, until the onions are clear and the shrimp turn pink. In a medium bowl, mix rice, shrimp and onion mix, French dressing diluted with white wine, Parmesan cheese, salt, pepper and chopped parsley. Toss until ingredients are just blended. Stuff each pepper with the rice mixture and place in a casserole dish lined with aluminum foil. Bake in a pre-heated 350 degrees oven for 25 minutes or until done. Yield: 4 peppers.

ROANOKE RICE WITH FRESH TOMATO

1	cup Jasmine, Basmati or long-grain rice
2	cups water
1	teaspoon salt
2	teaspoons vegetable oil, divided
½	cup chopped onion
½	cup chopped green pepper
1	clove minced garlic
2	medium fresh tomatoes, peeled and diced

In a medium saucepan, combine rice, water, salt and 1 teaspoon vegetable oil. Bring to a boil on medium heat. Reduce heat and simmer uncovered until most of water is absorbed. Cover and remove from heat. (Rice will continue to cook to the firm and fluffy stage).

In a larger saucepan, saute onion, pepper and garlic in remaining 1 teaspoon of oil, till soft. Add chopped tomatoes with their juice and heat through. Remove from heat and add cooked rice. Toss to combine. Serves 4.

Vegetables & Casseroles

ROASTED RED PEPPERS

Preheat broiler or prepare barbecue grill. Discard stems, seeds, and ribs from red bell peppers and place, skin side 2 inches from heat source. Cook, turning, until well charred (blackened) on all sides; 12-15 minutes. Place the charred peppers in a paper bag; close tightly and let stand for 10 minutes or more. Peel peppers and cut into pieces or strips, as desired. Can be used on salads, in pasta dishes or served marinated as part of an appetizer. (Recipe follows).

ROASTED RED PEPPERS, MARINATED

6-8 roasted red bell peppers (can be mixed with green and yellow)
1 clove garlic, minced
extra-virgin olive oil
fresh oregano sprigs, or dried oregano
salt and pepper to taste

Arrange roasted peppers in a serving dish. Sprinkle with garlic, drizzle with olive oil and garnish with oregano. Chill and right before serving, season with salt and pepper to taste. Makes a wonderful appetizer served over Mozzarella cheese. Yield: about 2 cups.

Note: To preserve these peppers, store in refrigerator with enough oil to cover them completely. They will last for several weeks. To serve, drain olive oil and save for making salad dressing.

SOUTHERN RICE

	vegetable cooking spray
1	cup sliced celery
¾	cup sliced green onions
¾	cup chopped green pepper
2¾	cups chicken broth
1	teaspoon poultry seasoning
½	teaspoon salt
⅛	teaspoon pepper
1½	cups long-grain rice, uncooked
¼	cup chopped pecans, toasted

Coat a large, non stick skillet with cooking spray; place over medium-high heat until hot. Add celery, green onions, and green pepper; saute until crisp-tender. Stir in broth, poultry seasoning, salt and pepper; bring to a boil.

Spoon rice into a shallow 2-quart baking dish; add hot broth mixture. Cover and bake at 350 degrees for 30 minutes or until rice is tender and liquid is absorbed. Sprinkle with pecans. Yield: 6 to 8 servings.

The best way to cook rice; bring long-grain white rice and double the amount of water to a boil. Reduce heat to low, cover and simmer 10 minutes. Remove covered pot from heat and let sit for 10 to 15 minutes more until all liquid is absorbed.

SOUTHPORT SWEET POTATO CROQUETTES

3	large sweet potatoes
⅓	cup sugar
2	tablespoons all-purpose flour
¼	teaspoon ground cinnamon
¼	teaspoon ground allspice
1	large egg, lightly beaten
18	large marshmallows
4	cups crushed cornflakes
	vegetable oil

Cook sweet potatoes in boiling water to cover 30 minutes or until tender. Drain and cool. Peel sweet potatoes, and mash.

Combine sugar, flour, cinnamon and allspice; stir with egg into mashed sweet potatoes. Shape mixture around marshmallows, and roll in crushed cereal; place in a single layer on a baking sheet. Cover and freeze 2 hours.

Pour oil into a large skillet to depth of ½ inch; heat to 350 degrees. Fry croquettes until golden brown, turning once. Serve immediately. Yield: 1½ dozen.

STUMPY POINT STUFFED SUMMER SQUASH

4	yellow crookneck squash
3	tablespoons unsalted butter, divided
½	cup minced yellow onions
¾	cup soft bread crumbs
1	large egg, well beaten
	cream or milk
	salt and black pepper to taste
¼	teaspoon each crumbled dried sage and thyme

Preheat oven to 350 degrees and position rack in center of oven. Trim ends of squash about ¼-inch. Slice in half the long way. With a melon-baller, remove the center pulp, carefully so as not to puncture the outer shell. Chop pulp and reserve in a mixing bowl. Saute the onions in 1 table-spoon butter in a saute pan over medium heat, until onions are transparent. Add the sauteed onions, bread crumbs and beaten egg to the chopped pulp and mix thoroughly. Moisten the filling mixture with a little milk or cream as necessary, keeping mixture fairly dry. Season with salt, pepper and herbs. Mix well.

Line a baking sheet with aluminum foil and arrange hollowed out squash shells, open side up so they do not touch. Spoon the filling into each, carefully packing to prevent air pockets. Mound the filling up on top and dot with remaining butter. Bake in the center of the oven until filling is set and tops are lightly browned—about 30 minutes. Serve hot. Yield 8 pieces.

Put your leftover rolls and bread crusts to good use by turning them into soft crumbs in your food processor and freezing in a zip-lock bag to use as needed. Freeze leftover pizza sauce or spaghetti sauce in ice cube trays. For a hot lunch or quick snack, pop out however many cubes you need. Thaw and heat the cubes of sauce; spread on an English muffin, and top with cheese for a quick mini pizza.

SWEET AND SOUR BRUSSELS SPROUTS

4	slices bacon, uncooked and diced
2	(10 ounce) packages brussel sprouts, thawed
¼	cup diced onion
¼	cup white vinegar
2	tablespoons sugar
1	teaspoon salt
1	teaspoon white pepper
¼	teaspoon dry mustard

Fry bacon crisp. Drain the bacon on paper towels. Leave bacon drippings in skillet.

Add brussel sprouts, onion, vinegar, sugar, salt, pepper and dry mustard. Stir and cover skillet. Cook over medium-high heat, stirring occasionally, about 10 minutes.

Stir in bacon and serve warm. Makes 6 servings.

TAR HEEL GREENS & BLACK-EYED PEAS

1   tablespoon olive oil
1   large onion, halved,sliced crosswise
2   cups diced ham (8 ounces)
4   large cloves garlic
1   can (14 ounce) diced, peeled tomatoes
1   box (10 ounce) frozen chopped turnip greens,
     (thawed, and squeezed dry)
1   cup chicken broth
¼   teaspoon crushed red pepper
¼   teaspoon salt
1   can (16 ounce) black-eyed peas, rinsed
2   teaspoons cider vinegar

Heat oil in large non-stick skillet. Add onion and saute over medium-high heat until golden, about 5 minutes. Add ham and saute over high heat 2 minutes until lightly browned. Add garlic: cook 1 minute until fragrant. Stir in tomatoes, turnip greens, chicken broth, crushed red pepper and salt. Bring to a boil, cover and simmer 10 minutes, stirring occasionally, until greens are tender.

Stir in peas and vinegar: heat through. Yield: 4 servings.

VEGETABLE MEDLEY ROMANO

3   cups zucchini slices
1   cup onion rings
3   tablespoons butter or margarine
1   cup tomatoes, chopped
     Romano cheese, grated

Saute zucchini and onion in butter or margarine 10 minutes. Add tomatoes; continue cooking over low heat 5 more minutes. Sprinkle generously with Romano cheese and serve. Serves 4.

WHALEBONE JUNCTION ROASTED POTATO WEDGES

 1 pound baking potatoes
 1 tablespoon canola oil
 2 teaspoons Cajun seasoning
  salt and pepper (optional)

Scrub and wash potatoes well, with a vegetable scrubbing brush. Cut each potato into wedges, leaving the skin on. In a large enough bowl to fit all the ingredients, blend the oil and seasoning together. Toss in the potato wedges and coat well. Spray a baking dish with vegetable spray to prevent sticking and add the seasoned potato wedges. Bake in a pre-heated 400 degrees oven for 25 -30 minutes or until tender. Season with salt and pepper if desired. Serves 4-6.

CELLA'S SAUSAGE, BROCCOLI AND TOMATO LASAGNA

½ cup packed sun-dried tomatoes (not in oil)
1¼ cups boiling water
2 large onions, chopped
3 tablespoons olive oil
1 pound hot Italian sausage, casings removed
2 tablespoons unsalted butter
3 tablespoons flour
1 cup milk
salt & pepper
1 bunch broccoli flowerettes, (about 4 cups)
12 7x3 ½" sheets dry no-boil lasagne pasta
10 ounces mozzarella, grated
1½ cups favorite cooked tomato sauce

In a small bowl, soak sun-dried tomatoes in boiling water 30 minutes. Strain over a bowl and reserve liquid. Chop tomatoes fine.

In a large non-stick skillet cook onions in 1 ½ tablespoons oil over moderate heat, stirring, until soft. Add sausage, stirring to break up, and simmer 5 minutes. Discard excess fat.

In a saucepan melt butter over moderately low heat and whisk in flour until smooth. Cook roux, whisking, 3 minutes. Add reserved soaking liquid and milk in a stream, whisking, add salt and pepper to taste and simmer, whisking occasionally, 5 minutes or until thick. Stir in sausage mixture and tomatoes.

In cleaned skillet heat remaining 1 ½ tablespoons oil over moderately high heat until hot but not smoking and saute broccoli, stirring until wilted. Add ¼ cup water and salt and pepper to taste. Simmer, covered partially, until broccoli is crisp-tender (about 2 minutes). Remove broccoli from skillet and set aside. Preheat oven to 375 degrees.

Pour 1 cup sausage sauce into a 13x9x2" baking dish and cover with 3 lasagne sheets, making sure they do not touch each other. Stir broccoli into remaining sausage sauce. Spread about 1 ½ cups sausage-broccoli sauce over pasta and sprinkle with ¾ cup mozzarella. Make 2 more layers in same manner, beginning and ending with pasta. Spread tomato sauce over pasta making sure pasta is completely covered and sprinkle with remaining mozzarella. Cover dish tightly with foil, tenting slightly to prevent foil from touching top layer, and bake in middle of oven 30 minutes. Remove foil and bake lasagne 10 minutes more, or until top is bubbling. Let lasagne stand 5 minutes before serving. Serves 8 as a main course.

BAKED ZITI WITH EGGPLANT

1	recipe marinara sauce (this section)
1	small eggplant
	salt & water for soaking eggplant slices
½	cup flour
½	teaspoon salt
⅛	teaspoon pepper
¼	cup milk
½	cup olive oil
1	(16-ounce) package ziti
1	(16-ounce) container ricotta cheese
2	eggs, slightly beaten
2	tablespoons fresh parsley, minced
2	tablespoons olive oil
1	(8-ounce) package part-skim mozzarella cheese
½	cup Parmesan cheese
	salt and pepper to taste

Prepare marinara sauce following recipe in this book. May be done a day ahead.

To prepare eggplant, rinse and slice into ¼" slices. Layer slices in a colander, sprinkling each layer with salt and water. Allow eggplant to drain for 30 minutes, removing the dark liquid and any possible bitter flavor.

Combine flour, ½ teaspoon salt and ⅛ teaspoon pepper in a shallow bowl; set aside. Place milk in a second shallow bowl. Heat olive oil in a heavy skillet.

Dipping eggplant slices in milk, then in flour mixture, saute each slice on one side until brown. Remove slices to a plate, and cut into wedges.

In a large pot, bring sufficient amount of water to a boil. Add ziti to water and bring to a second boil. Cook ziti about 4 minutes; pasta will be firm (semi-cooked). While ziti cooks, combine ricotta cheese, eggs and parsley. Stir gently to blend. Drain pasta when ready, running cold water over to stop the cooking process. Place cooled ziti in a bowl, and toss with olive oil.

To assemble ziti and eggplant casserole, pour 1 cup marinara sauce into the bottom of a lasagna pan. Layer ingredients as follows: ziti, cooked eggplant, ricotta cheese mixture, and half of the mozzarella cheese. Ladle sauce over each layer. (Note: there will be leftover sauce for table-use.) Bake casserole in a 350 degrees oven for 30 minutes. Remove and sprinkle top with reserved mozzarella cheese, Parmesan cheese and salt and pepper to taste. Bake an additional 10 minutes, or until cheese is lightly browned and bubbly. Serve with remaining marinara sauce and Italian bread. Yields: 8-10 servings.

BEAUFORT BAKED BEANS

½ cup firmly packed brown sugar
⅓ cup prepared mustard
¼ cup molasses
3 cans (about 16 ounces each) pinto beans, drained
1 sweet green pepper, chopped
1 sweet red pepper, chopped
1 medium-size onion, chopped

In medium-size bowl, mix together brown sugar, mustard and molasses until smooth. Stir brown sugar mixture with beans, green and red peppers and onion. Pour beans into a two-quart baking dish. Bake, uncovered in a pre-heated 350 degrees oven for about 1 hour and fifteen minutes or until slightly thickened. Yield: 8 servings.

BODIE ISLAND BREAKFAST CASSEROLE

3	cups frozen hash brown potatoes
¾	cup shredded Cheddar cheese
1	cup diced ham or breakfast sausage
¼	cup sliced green onion
4	beaten eggs
1	(12-ounce) can evaporated milk
¼	teaspoon pepper
⅛	teaspoon salt

Grease a 2-quart square baking dish. Arrange potatoes evenly in bottom of the dish. Sprinkle with cheese, ham, and green onion.

In a medium mixing bowl combine eggs, milk, pepper, and salt. Pour egg mixture over potatoes in dish. (Dish may be refrigerated at this point overnight). Bake, uncovered at 350 degrees for 45-50 minutes. Serves six.

CARIBBEAN RED BEANS AND RICE

1½	tablespoons canola oil
1	medium onion, chopped
2	cloves garlic, minced
2	cups diced pumpkin or squash
2½	teaspoons curry powder
½	teaspoon pepper
½	teaspoon salt
¼	teaspoon ground cloves
3	cups water
1½	cups long-grain rice
1	cup chopped kale
1	can red beans, drained

In a large saucepan, heat oil. Add onion and garlic; saute until soft. Stir in pumpkin (or squash) and seasonings and cook 1 minute. Add water and rice and cover. Cook 15 minutes. Stir in kale and beans. Cook 5 minutes more. Turn off heat, and fluff rice. Let stand for 10 to 15 minutes before serving. Yield: 6 servings.

Vegetables & Casseroles

CRAB, SHRIMP & ARTICHOKE AU GRATIN

4	cups water
1	pound unpeeled medium-size fresh shrimp
1	package frozen artichoke hearts (9 ounce)
1	can (6 ounce) lump crabmeat, rinsed and drained
2	cups shredded, sharp Cheddar cheese, divided
1	clove garlic, minced
2	tablespoons green onions, sliced
½	pound fresh mushrooms, sliced
¼	cup plus 2 tablespoons butter or margerine, divided
¼	cup all-purpose flour
¾	cup half-and-half
1	teaspoon dillweed
½	teaspoon pepper
⅔	cup dry white wine
2	tablespoons corn flakes, crushed
1½	teaspoons butter or margarine, melted

Bring water to a boil: add shrimp, cook 3 to 5 minutes. Drain and rinse with cold water. Peel and devein shrimp; set aside.

Cook artichoke hearts according to directions; drain. Combine artichokes, shrimp, crabmeat and 1 cup shredded Cheddar cheese in a large bowl; set mixture aside.

Saute garlic, green onions and mushrooms in 2 tablespoons butter until tender; drain. Stir the sauteed vegetables into shrimp mixture.

Melt ¼ cup butter in a large heavy skillet over low heat; add flour, stirring until smooth. Cook 1 minute, stirring constantly. Gradually add half-and-half; cook over medium heat, stirring until thickened and bubbly. Remove from heat; stir in dillweed, pepper, and remaining 1 cup cheese, stirring until cheese melts.

Gradually stir in wine. Cook sauce over medium heat, stirring constantly until thickened. Add shrimp mixture and stir again. Spoon into a lightly-greased shallow 2-quart baking dish; cover and chill 8 hours.

To bake, let stand at room temperature 30 minutes. Combine corn flakes crumbs and 1 ½ teaspoons butter; sprinkle over the casserole. Bake, uncovered, 350 degrees for 45 minutes. Yield 6 to 8 servings.

Vegetables & Casseroles

EMERALD ISLE CRAB AND SPINACH QUICHE

1	prepared 9" pastry shell
1	package frozen (10 ounce) chopped spinach
2	eggs, lightly beaten
1	container (8 ounce) plain yogurt
1	tablespoon all-purpose flour
1	teaspoon salt
¼	teaspoon pepper
1	can (6 ounce) crabmeat, well drained and flaked
½	cup fresh mushroom sauteed in 1 teaspoon butter
1	cup (4 ounce) shredded mild Cheddar cheese
¼	cup chopped onion

Preheat oven to 425 degrees. Cook spinach following package directions. Drain and squeeze out excess water. In a medium bowl, beat eggs with yogurt, flour, salt and pepper. Stir in crabmeat and spinach. Sprinkle mushrooms, cheese and onion over crust. Pour in spinach-crabmeat mixture. Bake in preheated 425 degree oven for 15 minutes. Lower heat to 350 degrees and bake 30 minutes more. Knife should come out clean when inserted in center. Yield: 6 servings.

HAMMOCK BEACH CHEESY MACARONI BAKE

1	package (8 ounce) uncooked elbow macaroni
1½	cups low-fat cottage cheese
1	cup shredded part-skim mozzarella cheese
1½	cups shredded sharp Cheddar cheese
1	large egg
¾	cup evaporated skim milk
2	tablespoons finely chopped onion
1	teaspoon Worcestershire sauce
½	teaspoon dry mustard
⅛	teaspoon white pepper
	dash paprika
1	teaspoon Parmesan cheese
½	cup toasted croutons

Preheat oven to 350 degrees. Cook macaroni according to package directions. Drain and set aside. In a large bowl, combine cottage, mozzarella and Cheddar cheeses with egg, milk, onion, Worcestershire sauce, mustard and white pepper. Mix until blended. Fold in cooked macaroni. Spoon mixture into a 2 ½-quart casserole dish sprayed with cooking spray and sprinkle with paprika and Parmesan cheese. Top with a handful of croutons. Bake 20 to 30 minutes, or until bubbly. Serves 8.

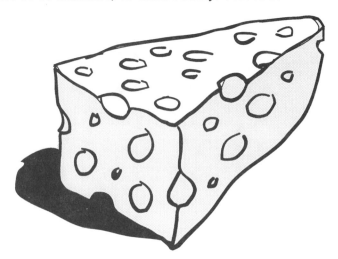

OCEAN ISLE OYSTER & EGG FRITTATA

1	tablespoon butter or margerine
⅓	cup sliced mushrooms
6	oysters, shucked and drained
1	tablespoon chopped green onion
1	slice bacon, cooked and crumbled
3	large eggs, beaten
	pinch each salt and freshly ground pepper
	chopped fresh parsley

Preheat oven to 400 degrees. Heat butter in 8-inch ovenproof non-stick skillet over medium heat. Add mushrooms and cook, stirring, until tender, 3 minutes. Add oysters, green onion and bacon; cook 30 seconds. Stir in eggs, salt and pepper. Lift sides of frittata with heat-resistant rubber spatula, letting liquid run over edges, until set. Transfer to oven and bake 3 to 5 minutes, just until top is barely dry. Sprinkle with parsley. Makes 1 serving.

ORIENTAL VEGETABLE LO MEIN

2	cups fresh snow pea pods, trimmed
1	cup red bell pepper strips
1	cup broccoli flowerets
½	cup shredded carrot
2	tablespoons chopped green onions
1	teaspoon grated fresh ginger
⅛	teaspoon dried crushed red pepper
2	cloves garlic, pressed
1	tablespoon vegetable oil
3	tablespoons soy sauce
1	tablespoon water
6	ounces vermicelli, cooked
1½	teaspoons sesame oil

In a large Non-stick skillet, stir-fry the vegetables with ginger, dried red pepper and garlic in vegetable oil for 2 minutes. Stir in soy sauce and water; add vermicelli and toss. Remove from heat, and toss with sesame oil. Serve with egg rolls, if desired. Yield: 3 to 4 servings.

PAELLA

½ cup olive oil
1 frying chicken, cut into small pieces
½ pound chorizo sausage
1 teaspoon paprika
1 medium-sized onion, chopped
2 celery stalks, chopped
2 cloves garlic, crushed
1½ cups uncooked rice
½ teaspoon saffron
3 cups chicken broth, divided
2 tomatoes, cut in slices or wedges
2 teaspoons salt
1 tablespoon parsley
½ teaspoon pepper
  dash cayenne pepper
1 large green pepper, chopped
1 pound shrimp, peeled and deveined
1 dozen small clams, washed and scrubbed
1½ dozen mussels, washed

In a large skillet or paella pan, pour in the olive oil and heat to medium-high. Cook chicken and sausage pieces until browned. Sprinkle with paprika and remove from pan, setting aside. Add onions and celery, cooking until just tender, about 3 minutes. Add garlic and rice; saute till rice is golden brown and coated with the oil. Add saffron and 2 tablespoons of the chicken broth, mixing and turning ingredients until blended. Pour in remaining broth, stirring as added. Add tomato, salt, parsley, cayenne and peppers. Place chicken and sausage pieces on top of mixture; bring to a boil and simmer until rice is tender (15-20 minutes). Stir several times during the cooking process. Add the shrimp, clams and mussels. Continue cooking until shrimp are done and clam and mussel shells open. (Discard any that do not!) This should require about 10 minutes cooking time. Serves 6.

PARRIS ISLAND PECAN RICE

1   cup extra long grain rice
2   cups chicken broth
½   cup onion, chopped
½   cup pecans, chopped
1   cup frozen peas, thawed
     black pepper

In a saucepan, combine rice, chicken broth and onion. Bring to a boil. Reduce the heat and simmer for 20 minutes, or until rice is cooked. Fold in pecans and peas. Sprinkle with pepper. Serves 6.

RIGATONI WITH FRESH TOMATO AND PEPPER

8   ounces rigatoni
1   tablespoon olive oil, divided
2   cloves garlic, chopped
2   cups julienned red, green and yellow bell peppers
1   cup fresh tomatoes, chopped
½   cup fresh basil, chopped
⅛   teaspoon ground black pepper
½   cup part-skim ricotta cheese
½   cup part-skim mozzarella cheese, shredded
1   tablespoon Parmesan cheese, grated

Cook pasta according to package directions. Drain, toss with 1 teaspoon olive oil and set aside.

Meanwhile, in a medium to large saute pan, heat remaining oil over medium heat. Add garlic and saute for 1 minute. Add peppers and saute 2 minutes. Add tomatoes and saute for 2 minutes more. Stir in basil, ground pepper, ricotta and mozzarella cheeses. Spoon over cooked pasta and sprinkle with Parmesan. Bake in a pre-heated 350 degrees oven for 15 minutes or until top of rigatoni is crispy. Yield: 4 side-dish servings.

SEASIDE SAUSAGE & CHEESE GRITS

1	cup quick-cooking yellow or white grits
2	cups sharp Cheddar cheese, shredded
¼	cup milk
2	tablespoons butter or margarine
2	teaspoons Worcestershire sauce
1½	teaspoons garlic salt
1	egg, beaten
1	pound hot bulk pork sausage, cooked and drained
1	cup sharp Cheddar cheese, shredded

Prepare quick-cooking grits according to package directions. Remove from heat and add 2 cups Cheddar cheese, milk, butter, Worcestershire sauce and garlic salt, stirring until cheese melts. Stir a small amount of grits mixture into beaten egg; add egg to remaining grits mixture, stirring constantly. Spoon half of grits mixture into a lightly greased 8-inch square baking dish; top with sausage. Spoon remaining grits mixture over sausage. Bake, uncovered at 350 degrees for 40 minutes. Sprinkle with 1 cup cheese, and bake an additional 5 minutes. Yield: 8 servings.

SPAGHETTI WITH MARINARA SAUCE

1	small onion, chopped
2	cloves garlic, diced
¼	cup olive oil
2	(28-ounce) cans Italian plum tomatoes
	salt and pepper to taste
2	teaspoons sugar
¼	cup dry white wine
½	cup chopped fresh parsley
2	tablespoons chopped fresh basil
¼	cup Parmesan cheese
12	ounces thin spaghetti, or other pasta

Saute onion and garlic in olive oil, until transparent. Add tomatoes, salt, pepper and sugar. Bring to a boil, add white wine, parsley and basil.

Reduce heat and simmer about 30 minutes or until liquid has cooked down. Shortly before sauce is finished, stir in Parmesan cheese. Adjust seasonings, remove from heat and let sit while spaghetti cooks.

Cook spaghetti according to package directions. Drain well. Serve sauce over spaghetti immediately. Makes 4 servings.

GRILLED ASPARAGUS FROM OAK HOLLOW ROAD

1   pound fresh asparagus
½   cup Italian salad dressing
     salt and pepper to taste

Wash asparagus gently and trim down tough, woody stems. Place asparagus in a bowl and using half of the salad dressing, marinate for at least one hour.

In the meantime, preheat grill to medium. When ready to cook, place asparagus in a grilling basket (or on a vegetable grid) and place this on the grill. Cook asparagus 4-5 minutes, then turn, cooking another 2-3 minutes or until done. Asparagus should be firm when cooked. Remove from heat and serve, using remaining dressing to brush on if desired. Salt and pepper to taste and serve. Yield: 4-6 servings.

Meat & Poultry

Meat & Poultry

APRICOT GRILLED LAMB KABOBS

½   cup teriyaki sauce
3   tablespoons apricot jam
1   tablespoon rice wine vinegar
1   teaspoon dried rosemary, crushed
2   teaspoons minced garlic
1   pound boneless lean lamb, cut into 1-inch pieces
1   large purple onion, quartered

In a small saucepan, bring teriyaki sauce, apricot jam, rice vinegar, rosemary and minced garlic to a boil, stirring constantly. Cool completely. Reserve ⅓ cup mixture.

Place lamb and onion in a shallow dish or large heavy-duty zip-top plastic bag; pour remaining teriyaki mixture over lamb. Cover or seal, and chill 1 hour, turning occasionally.

Remove lamb and onion from marinade, discarding marinade. Alternate lamb and onion on 4 (8-inch) skewers.

Coat food rack with cooking spray; place on grill over medium-high heat (350 degrees - 400 degrees). Place kabobs on rack, and grill, covered with grill lid, 8 minutes or to desired degree of doneness, turning and basting occasionally with reserved teriyaki mixture. Yield: 4 servings.

BACON-WRAPPED FILET MIGNON

¼   teaspoon salt
⅛   teaspoon pepper
4   filet mignon steaks about 1 inch thick
1   tablespoon dried Italian seasoning
2   slices bacon

Prepare grill or broiler pan. Sprinkle salt and pepper on steaks. Rub with Italian seasoning. Cut bacon in half lengthwise; wrap half around each filet; secure with a wooden toothpick. Grill or broil, 6 inches from heat 8-10 minutes, turning once (150 degrees for medium-rare). Remove to serving platter; let stand 5 minutes and serve. Yield: 4 steaks.

BARBECUED SAUSAGE WITH
PEPPER AND ONION

6   pork (or beef) sausages
2   onions, cut in wedges
1   large red bell pepper
1   large green bell pepper
    oil for brushing
    crusty French bread

Prick the sausages with a fork in several places, to allow the excess fat to run out during cooking. Place onion wedges in a grilling basket. Slice peppers in wedges and add to the onions. Brush sausages and vegetables with oil. Place sausages on hot grill and cook, turning, about 10 minutes or until done. Add vegetables in the grilling basket the last 5 minutes. Serve sausages together with grilled peppers and onions over crusty French bread. Serves 6.

BEEF TENDERLOIN DEL MAR

6   green onions, chopped
½   cup butter or margarine, melted
3   beef-flavored bouillon cubes
2   tablespoons red wine vinegar
1   (5 to 6 pound) beef tenderloin, trimmed

Saute green onions in butter in a small saucepan until tender; add beef-flavored bouillon cubes, stirring until dissolved; remove from heat, and stir in vinegar.

Place tenderloin in a large, shallow dish. Spoon butter mixture over top; cover and let stand at room temperature 15 minutes.

Place tenderloin on a rack in a roasting pan; insert meat thermometer into thickest portion of tenderloin. Bake at 425 degrees for 30 to 45 minutes or until thermometer registers 140 degrees (rare) or 160 degrees (medium). Let stand 10 minutes before slicing. Yield: 8 to 10 servings.

CAROLINA BARBECUED RIBS

1   cup water
4   pounds spareribs, cut into serving pieces
1   cup favorite NC prepared barbecue sauce

Place water and ribs in Slow Cooker; cover. Turn heat control to LOW. Cook 6 to 8 hours or until meat is tender. Drain ribs and place on broiling pan. Brush all sides generously with barbecue sauce. Broil 4 to 6 inches from heat until browned, turning once, 15 to 20 minutes. Makes 4 to 6 servings.

When ribs are on sale, buy several racks of them and cut into cooking-size portions. Bake ribs; cool, then wrap and freeze. When ribs are on the menu, thaw them and grill directly over medium coals for 10 to 15 minutes, turning once to baste with favorite barbeque sauce.

CHEF'S BEST MEAT LOAF - BBQ - STYLE

    3   slices day-old bread
    ½   cup fresh parsley, chopped
    1   pound chopped beef, pork and veal
    ½   teaspoon garlic salt
    ½   teaspoon freshly ground pepper
    ½   cup favorite smokey-flavored BBQ sauce
    1   egg, lightly beaten

Break bread into 1-inch pieces and place in a food processor. Process into coarse bread crumbs. Add parsely and process briefly to blend.

Add the meat loaf mixture to the breadcrumbs and sprinkle the seasonings over the meat. Saving about 2 tablespoons, add the BBQ sauce. Pulse and process until mixture starts to blend. While pulsing, add the egg through the feed tube and blend until all ingredients are mixed and smooth. Turn meat out onto work surface and with moistened hands, form meat into a loaf. Place into a 1-pound bread pan and spread remaining 2 tablespoons of BBQ sauce over top.

Bake in a pre-heated 350 degrees oven 50 - 60 minutes depending on the shape of your loaf. Cool 10 minutes before turning out of pan. Yield: 4 servings.

Mixing together a meat loaf is a snap when you use a pastry blender to combine ingredients. Your hands stay clean this way.

CRISPY RIBS WITH PLUM SAUCE

5 pounds spare ribs
3 pounds fresh plums, cut into wedges
3 tablespoons soy sauce
1½ tablespoons cornstarch
1½ tablespoons sugar
2 teaspoons grated fresh ginger
2 cloves garlic, minced

Cut spareribs into 6 sections, and place in a single layer in a large roasting pan. Bake ribs, covered, at 350 degrees for 30 minutes.

Process plum wedges in a blender or food processor until smooth, stopping once to scrape down sides. Bring plum puree, soy sauce, cornstarch, sugar, ginger and cloves to a boil in a heavy saucepan over medium-high heat; boil, stirring constantly, 8-10 minutes or until mixture is thick and clear.

Reserve half of sauce for dipping; brush ribs with half of remaining sauce. Grill ribs, over medium heat (300 degrees to 350 degrees) about 30 minutes or until done, turning after each 6 - 8 minutes, and brushing with remaining basting sauce. Serve ribs with reserved dipping sauce. Yield: 6 servings.

GARLIC-RUBBED T-BONE STEAK

3 cloves garlic, finely chopped
¼ teaspoon salt
1 T-bone steak, well trimmed (1½ pounds, 1-inch thick)
1 teaspoon coarsely ground black pepper
    parsley for garnish

On a cutting board, add half the salt to garlic; mash to a paste with side of knife. Sprinkle steak with remaining salt. Rub garlic paste on both sides of steak. Press pepper into steak. Cover; refrigerate for 1 hour. Coat broiler pan with cooking spray.

Heat broiler. Broil steak 6 inches from heat for 12 to 15 minutes, turning once, for medium-rare (150 degrees). Remove to serving platter and garnish with parsley. Serves 4.

GRILLED HAM STEAK WITH APPLE-MUSTARD SAUCE

1	center-cut ham steak, (about 2 pounds)
½	cup firmly packed brown sugar
⅓	cup apple juice
2	tablespoons prepared sharp mustard
¼	teaspoon cinnamon
⅛	teaspoon nutmeg
⅛	teaspoon ground cloves

Trim excess fat from steak; score remaining fat at 1-inch intervals.

Prepare coals, or set electric or gas grill to medium. Grill ham steak 12-14 minutes, turning once.

While ham steak grills, combine sugar, apple juice, mustard and spices in a small metal saucepan with a flameproof handle. Heat on grill, stirring several times, until bubbly-hot. Baste ham with heated mixture; grill 5 minutes, turn and baste again; grill 5 minutes longer, or until well glazed. Yield: 6 servings.

GRILLED MARINATED FLANK STEAK

2	tablespoons vegetable oil
2	tablespoons balsamic vinegar
2	tablespoons favorite barbecue sauce
1	tablespoon Worcestershire sauce
¼	cup whole, black peppercorns
2	garlic cloves, peeled
1	tablespoon lemon juice
1	1 ½ pound flank steak

Place vegetable oil, vinegar, barbecue sauce, Worcestershire sauce, peppercorns, garlic cloves and lemon juice in a blender. Process until smooth, stopping once to scrape down sides.

Place steak in a shallow dish and pour mixture over to marinate. Cover and chill at least 3 hours.

Remove steak from marinade, discarding marinade. Grill, with lid down, over medium-high heat, 7 minutes on each side, or to desired degree of doneness. Yield: 6 servings.

Meat & Poultry

MURRELL'S INLET VEAL AND PEPPERS

1	pound veal (your choice) chops, cutlets or stew meat
2	tablespoons vegetable oil
2	onions, sliced
3	teaspoons paprika
3	tablespoons all-purpose flour
⅛	teaspoon pepper
1¼	cup beef broth
¾	teaspoon Worcestershire sauce
2	carrots, cut in ½-inch pieces
1	green pepper, chopped
3	cups hot, cooked rice
3	tablespoons chopped parsley

Over medium-high heat, in a 5-quart Dutch oven, heat oil and brown veal on all sides. Remove and drain on paper towels. Set aside.

Reduce heat to medium. Saute onion and paprika 5 minutes. Stir in flour and ⅛ teaspoon of pepper; add broth, Worcestershire, carrots and veal. Bring to boiling; simmer 30 minutes, or until veal and carrots are tender.

Stir in green pepper; simmer 5 minutes, or until tender. Toss rice with parsley; serve with veal. Serves 5-6.

When freezing purchased meat, always remove meat from store wrapper. It is thin and porous and not meant for long term use. Re-wrap meat in heavy-duty freezer paper or plastic wrap. Seal with freezer tape. And don't forget to date.

Always defrost meat in refrigerator, not on the kitchen counter top. Warm temperatures promote the growth of bacteria.

NORTH CAROLINA STYLE PULLED-PORK-BARBECUE

1   loin of pork roast (about 6 pounds)
3   cups distilled white vinegar
1   cup water
2   tablespoons hot pepper sauce
1   tablespoon prepared yellow mustard
1   tablespoon salt

To bake: heat oven to 400 degrees. Place roast in baking pan; cover with aluminum foil. Bake in 400 degrees oven for 30 minutes; reduce oven temperature to 325 degrees. Bake another 3 hours or until fork slips easily into meat. When cool enough to handle, shred meat; place in a bowl.

To grill: prepare gas grill. Turn half of grill on high, leaving the other half off. Add water-soaked mesquite or hickory chips to side that is turned on. Place roast on side that is off. Grill, covered, until fork slips easily into meat and instant-read thermometer placed in thickest part of roast reads 170 degrees , about 2 hours. Cook slowly, so meat doesn't burn on outside. When meat is cool enough to handle, shred meat and place in bowl.

Meanwhile, stir together vinegar, water, hot sauce, mustard and salt in a medium bowl. Stir about 1 ½ cups vinegar sauce into meat. Serve on split buns with remaining sauce on side. Serve with coleslaw. Yield: 12 servings.

NOTE: This recipe is a great crowd pleaser and a real tradition on the beaches in North Carolina.

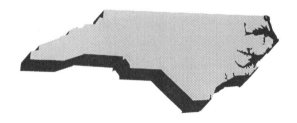

PORK TENDERLOIN WITH MUSTARD SAUCE

4	pork tenderloins (about 4 pounds)
½	cup soy sauce
½	cup dry white wine
¼	cup brown sugar
½	cup sour cream
½	cup mayonnaise
1	tablespoon dry mustard
1	tablespoon chopped onions
1½	tablespoons white wine vinegar

In a shallow dish, marinate tenderloins in blend of soy sauce, wine and brown sugar. Let stand in refrigerator 2 hours or more, turning occasionally to coat all sides of meat.

To prepare the mustard sauce, mix sour cream, mayonnaise, mustard, onions and vinegar in a medium bowl. Let stand at room temperature for one hour. Refrigerate until one hour prior to grilling. At this time, remove tenderloins from refrigerator and let sit. Prepare grill to cook at a low temperature. Grill tenderloins on LOW, basting and turning, until meat is browned nicely on outside and cooked through. Approximate cooking time of about 12 to 15 minutes will vary with each barbecue grill. Serve with mustard sauce. Yield: 6 servings.

SOUTH RIVER THREE-PEPPPER STRIP STEAK

2	boneless New York strip steaks, 1¼" thick
1	tablespoon ground lemon-pepper
1	teaspoon ground cardamom
2	tablespoons butter
4	teaspoons olive oil
2	teaspoons fresh grated lemon rind
2	tablespoons sliced green onion tops
1	cup mixed pepper strips (red, green, yellow)
1	tablespoon rice vinegar
1	tablespoon soy sauce

Combine lemon pepper and cardamom, sprinkle over steak, lightly rub into beef. Let stand 10 minutes. Heat butter, oil and lemon rind in large, heavy frying pan over medium-high heat until hot. Add steaks, pan grill 8 to 10 minutes, turning once. Remove steaks to heated platter. Add onion tops, peppers, rice vinegar and soy sauce to frying pan. Stir-fry over high heat for 30 seconds and serve over steak. Serves 2.

SPICY HURRICANE HAMBURGERS

1	pound ground beef
2	teaspoons Old Bay Seasoning
4	slices sharp Cheddar cheese
4	hamburger buns
	salt and pepper if desired

Mix the seasoning with the ground beef. Divide into four balls, and form hamburger patties. Heat coals or gas grill. Spray grilling rack with vegetable spray to prevent hamburgers from sticking. Grill, turning once until medium-well. (180 degrees on meat thermometer). During the last seconds of grilling, top with Cheddar cheese slices. Season with salt and pepper (optional), and serve on hamburger buns. Serves 4.

SWEET AND TART PAMLICO PORK MEDALLIONS

2	pork tenderloins (¾ to 1 pound)
	garlic pepper blend
4	teaspoons butter
4	tablespoon green onions, finely chopped
¾	cup chicken broth (more, if necessary)
4	teaspoons dijon-style mustard
2	tablespoons maple syrup
2	tablespoons balsamic vinegar

Slice the pork tenderloins into 1-inch slices. With the heel of your hand, gently flatten pork slices to a thickness of about ¼-inch. Season both sides of medallions with seasoned pepper blend.

In a large, heavy skillet, heat butter over medium-high heat. Cook medallions for 3 to 4 minutes per side, turning once, until nicely browned. Remove medallions; keeping warm.

Add onions to skillet; cook and stir for 30 seconds. Stir in chicken broth and mustard. Cook, uncovered, for 2 minutes, stirring; stir in maple syrup and vinegar. Continue cooking, uncovered, for a minute more, until sauce thickens slightly.

Return pork to skillet; heat through; serve medallions with pan sauce. Makes 4 servings.

BEER AND MUSTARD GRILLED TURKEY

2	pounds turkey tenderloins
½	cup light beer
½	cup honey mustard salad dressing
½	teaspoon cracked pepper
2	cloves garlic, crushed

Combine beer, salad dressing, pepper and garlic in a large zip-lock top bag. Mix well. Add turkey and marinate in refrigerator for 20 minutes to 2 hours. Remove turkey from marinade. Grill over hot coals about 30 minutes until meat is no longer pink in the center or meat thermometer inserted in deepest part of meat reads 170 degrees. Let stand 10 minutes before slicing. Serve with Honey Mustard salad dressing as a sauce. Serves 8.

CAJUN CHICKEN BREAST HALVES WITH GUACAMOLE

4   skinless, boned chicken breast halves
$\frac{1}{4}$ cup butter, melted

BLACKENING SPICE MIX as follows:
1   teaspoon salt
1   tablespoon sweet paprika
1   teaspoon dried onion granules
1   teaspoon dried garlic
1   teaspoon dried thyme
1   teaspoon cayenne
$\frac{1}{2}$ teaspoon cracked, black pepper
$\frac{1}{2}$ teaspoon dried oregano
Recipe for Guacamole (this book)

Put each chicken breast between 2 pieces of plastic wrap and pound with a mallet or rolling pin until they are ½ inch thick. Brush each chicken breast all over with melted butter. Set aside.

Combine the spice mix ingredients in a shallow bowl. Coat the chicken breasts with the spice mix, insuring that they are covered completely. Set aside. Place the chicken breast halves over the hottest part of a very hot barbecue, and cook for 8-10 minutes, turning once. Slice the breasts into thick pieces, and serve immediately with the guacamole. Serves 4.

To eliminate any possible contamination from poultry, always cook thoroughly.

CAROLINA'S BEST FRIED CHICKEN

3	quarts water
1	tablespoon salt
1	(2-2½ pound) whole chicken, cut up
1	teaspoon salt
1	teaspoon pepper
1	cup all-purpose flour
2	cups vegetable oil
¼	cup bacon drippings

Combine the water and salt in large bowl; add chicken and refrigerate 8 hours or overnight.

Drain chicken and pat dry. In a zip-lock bag, combine salt, pepper and flour. Place 2 pieces of chicken in the bag at a time and shake to coat with flour. When all chicken pieces are flour-coated, combine oil and bacon drippings in and electric frying pan. Heat to 360 degrees. Add chicken, and cook until both sides are golden brown (about 25 minutes). Remove and drain on paper towels. Yield: 4 servings.

CHERRY GROVE CHICKEN AND DUMPLINGS

¾   cup flour
     whole chicken, cut up
     canola oil for sauteing
2   small onions, quartered
1   cup sliced carrots
1   pint chicken stock
1   bay leaf
1   cup flour
1   teaspoon baking powder
¼   teaspoon salt
¾   cup milk
3   tablespoons canola oil
     salt & freshly ground pepper

Lightly flour the chicken pieces and saute in small amount of oil, until lightly browned. Add onions, cooking until they color slightly. Add carrots, stock and bay leaf; cover and simmer 30 minutes.

Mix the flour, baking powder and salt. Stir in milk and oil.

When carrots, onions and chicken are tender, taste broth and season with salt and pepper to taste. Remove bay leaf.

Drop 1-inch spoonfuls of batter into chicken and vegetables. Cover, bring to boil and simmer 10 to 15 minutes. Dumplings will be fluffy and double in size when done. Serve with rice. Serves 4.

After stewing a chicken for diced meat for casseroles, etc., let cool in broth before removing from bone. It will have twice the flavor.

CHERRY POINT CHICKEN TOSTADAS

1	pound skinned and boned chicken breast halves
½	cup fresh lime juice
4	(8-inch) flour tortillas
½	teaspoon salt
¼	teaspoon pepper
	vegetable oil
1	cup picante sauce
2	tablespoons fresh cilantro, finely chopped
2	tablespoons sour cream
4	cups shredded lettuce
2	medium tomatoes, chopped
6	fresh mushrooms, sliced

Cut chicken into ¾-inch cubes and place in a shallow dish or heavy-duty, zip-top plastic bag. Pour lime juice over chicken; cover and refrigerate 30 minutes.

Place tortillas on a baking sheet; bake at 350 degrees for 3 to 5 minutes or until lightly browned and crisp. Set aside.

Remove chicken from lime juice, discarding lime juice. Sprinkle chicken with salt and pepper.

Coat a skillet lightly with oil, and heat over medium flame. Add chicken, and cook, stirring often, 4 minutes or until done. Stir in picante sauce, cilantro, and sour cream. Return to a simmer, and cook, stirring occasionally, 5 minutes.

Place tortillas on serving plates; spoon chicken mixture evenly onto tortillas; top with lettuce, tomato and mushrooms. Cut into wedges, and serve immediately. Yield: 4 servings.

Meat & Poultry

COUNTRY STYLE CHICKEN POT PIE

2	pounds cooked chicken meat
1	medium onion, chopped
2-3	ribs celery, chopped
8	tablespoons butter or margarine, divided
¾	cup flour (for roux)
3	cups chicken broth
½	cup green peas, thawed
½	cup sliced cooked carrots
3	cups biscuit mix
	desired amount of salt and pepper

Heat oven to 350 degrees. Dice chicken and set aside. Saute onions and celery in 1 tablespoon butter; set aside. Melt remaining butter over medium-low heat. Blend in flour, and continue cooking, stirring, until roux bubbles. Whisk in chicken broth. When roux is incorporated, bring to a slow boil. Reduce heat and continue whisking until sauce thickens, about 5 minutes. Stir in chicken, peas and carrots; season to taste, if desired and set aside.

Prepare biscuit mix according to package directions. Roll out enough dough to cover 6 individual casseroles. Spoon chicken mixture into baking dishes. Cover each with dough. Crimp edges and pierce dough with a fork. Bake 45 minutes to 1 hour or until crust is golden. Makes 6 pies.

DUCK BREASTS GRILLED WITH ORANGE, GINGER AND BALSAMIC SAUCE

	duck breasts to yield 4 servings (small or large birds)
½	cup fresh orange juice
1½	cups chicken stock
3	tablespoons balsamic vinegar
2	teaspoons freshly grated ginger
4	tablespoons unsalted butter
½	teaspoon salt
1	teaspoon cracked black peppercorns
	zest from 1 small orange

Prepare outdoor barbecue, gas or electric grill. Clean and wash breasts, pat dry and set aside.

Combine orange juice and stock in a medium saucepan over medium-high heat. Reduce by one-half, about 15-20 minutes, uncovered. Add balsamic vinegar and ginger, cook 2-3 minutes, then add butter, 1 tablespoon at a time while whisking constantly. After butter is completely integrated, add salt, pepper and orange zest. Turn off heat, cover and keep warm.

When ready to grill, lay breasts on grate. Grill 6-8 minutes, turn and grill about 8 minutes more, or until the meat is medium-rare. (Time will vary depending on the type of duck breast used.) Transfer duck breasts to a wooden cutting board and slice thinly on the bias. Fan out on warm plates and ladle with a generous amount of sauce. Yield: 4 servings.

If purchasing poultry to freeze, always freeze immediately.

HONEY GRILLED CHICKEN WINGS

¾   cup honey
¼   cup white wine Worcestershire sauce
½   teaspoon ground ginger
16-20 chicken wings (or 3 pounds)

Mix honey, Worcestershire sauce and ginger. Grill wings on heated coals or gas grill on medium heat for 20 to 25 minutes, brushing frequently with honey mixture and turning once until wings are cooked crispy. Serves 4.

JAMAICAN JERK CHICKEN

3   scallions, finely chopped
1   medium yellow onion, chopped
1   or 2 jalapeno peppers, seeded and minced
2   tablespoons vegetable oil
2   tablespoons soy sauce
1   tablespoon fresh lime juice
3   garlic cloves, minced
1   tablespoon light brown sugar
1   teaspoon thyme
¾   teaspoon ground cinnamon
¼   teaspoon ground nutmeg
1   teaspoon ground allspice
1   teaspoon salt
2   pounds chicken breasts, skinless, boneless and pounded

Combine all ingredients except chicken in a blender or food processor. Process for 10 to 15 seconds at high speed. Pour the marinade over the chicken in a shallow bowl, and refrigerate at least 4 hours or overnight.

When ready to cook, remove the chicken from the marinade and place on baking sheets. Bake at 375 degrees for 25-30 minutes, or until chicken is cooked.

To grill, remove the chicken from the marinade and place on pre-heated, lightly-oiled grill. Cook for about 7 minutes on each side or until chicken is cooked. Yield: 6 servings.

LANDLUBBER'S LIGHT & LEMONY CHICKEN

⅔	cup chicken broth
1	teaspoon soy sauce
1	teaspoon grated lemon peel
¼	cup lemon juice
1	tablespoon sugar
1	tablespoon corn starch
	dash pepper
4	boneless, skinless chicken breast halves
8	green onions, sliced
2	cups frozen baby carrots
1	pound fresh asparagus spears, cut into 1-inch pieces

In a small bowl combine broth, soy sauce, lemon peel, lemon juice, sugar, cornstarch, and pepper; mix well and set aside

Cut chicken into bite-size strips. Coat a large non-stick skillet or wok with cooking spray and heat over high heat until hot. Add chicken and onions; cook and stir until chicken is lightly browned and no longer pink. Remove skillet from heat; place chicken and onions on plate.

Spray skillet again with cooking spray. Heat over high heat about 1 minute. Add carrots and asparagus; cook and stir 3 or 4 minutes or until crisp-tender. Return chicken and onions to skillet. Stir sauce well; pour over chicken and vegetables. Cook and stir just until sauce thickens. Serve over cooked white rice. Serves 4.

Coat skinless chicken breast halves with flour to prevent the outside from getting tough and stringy, and keep the inside juicey.

PAMLICO PECAN CRUSTED CHICKEN

2	cups pecans, finely ground
1	cup yellow cornmeal
5	cloves garlic, minced
2	tablespoons gingerroot, minced
1	teaspoon ground black pepper
2	tablespoons salt
3	cups all-purpose flour, divided
2	cups buttermilk
8	chicken breast halves

Heat oven to 350 degrees. Combine the ground pecans, cornmeal, garlic, gingerroot, pepper, salt and 1 cup flour in a medium bowl. Place remaining flour and buttermilk in separate bowls.

Dredge chicken in flour, dip in buttermilk and roll in pecan mixture. Bake chicken, covered with foil, 15 minutes in a greased, shallow baking dish. Carefully remove foil and bake another 20-25 minutes or until chicken is golden brown.

Remove chicken from baking dish and cool. Chicken will become crisp as it cools. Makes 8 servings.

QUAIL GRILLED WITH BLACKBERRY SAUCE

2 (14-ounce) packages quail, dressed with breasts deboned
1 (8-ounce) bottle Italian dressing
½ cup dry red wine
1 (10-ounce) jar seedless blackberry spread

Rinse quail and pat dry. Place in a large shallow dish and add Italian dressing. Cover or seal, and chill at least 8 hours.

When ready to cook, remove quail, discarding marinade.

Cook wine in a small saucepan over medium heat 5 minutes or until reduced by half. Whisk in blackberry spread until smooth. Reserve ¾ cup.

Grill quail over medium heat (300 degrees to 350 degrees) 15 minutes, turning once and basting with remaining blackberry sauce. Serve with reserved ¾ cup sauce. Yield: serves 4.

SURF CITY SESAME GRILLED CHICKEN

⅓ cup vegetable oil
¼ cup white vinegar
1 tablespoon sesame seeds, toasted
½ teaspoon sugar
1 teaspoon sesame oil
4 boneless, skinless chicken breast halves

Mix vegetable oil, vinegar, sesame seeds, sugar and sesame oil together in a medium bowl. Beat with a wire whisk until well blended. Add chicken breast halves and let marinate for 30 minutes. Meantime, heat coals or gas grill. Grill chicken 4 to 6 inches from medium heat 15 to 20 minutes or until done, basting and turning once. Serves 4.

Seafood

BAKED ROCKFISH OUTER BANKS STYLE

⅓ cup minced onion
3 tablespoons butter
½ pound fresh lump crab meat
½ cup fresh bread crumbs
¼ cup fresh chopped parsley
¼ cup heavy cream
1 teaspoon thyme
¼ teaspoon lemon pepper
4-pound striped bass, dressed for stuffing
salt and pepper
⅓ cup dry wine
⅓ cup melted butter

Saute onion in butter until golden. Remove from heat and mix in the crab meat, bread crumbs, parsley, heavy cream, thyme and lemon pepper. Stuff the fish and skewer the edges securely. Place fish in a greased baking pan and pour the wine mixed with the melted butter over the fish. Bake in a pre-heated 400 degrees oven, uncovered for 30 minutes, or just until the flesh is opaque, basting frequently with the wine-butter mixture. Serves 4 to 6.

BALD HEAD ISLAND CRAB RAVIOLI

1   pound fresh or frozen lump crabmeat, thawed and drained
1   (8-ounce) package. cream cheese, softened
⅔   cup chopped leek
2   tablespoons chopped fresh chives
2   tablespoons finely diced onion
2   tablespoons white wine
1   teaspoon Worcestershire sauce
48   wonton wrappers (may be purchased in your supermarket)

Pick through crab meat, removing any bits of shell particles; set aside. In a medium bowl, blend together cream cheese, chopped leek, chives, onion, wine and Worcestershire sauce. Gently stir in the crab meat.

For each ravioli, place a rounded tablespoon of crab filling in center of a wonton wrapper. Brush edges with water and place a second wrapper over first, pressing to seal edges. Trim with a fluted pastry wheel, if desired. Repeat with remaining wrappers and filling.

In a large Dutch oven cook the ravioli in 2 batches, in a large amount of gently boiling, lightly salted water 2 to 2 ½ minutes or just until tender. (Do not boil water too vigorously.)

Using a slotted spoon, remove the ravioli as they are done. Place in a single layer on lightly greased baking sheet. Cover loosely with foil. Keep warm in a 300 degrees oven up to 20 minutes, while cooking remaining ravioli. Serve as soon as possible, with your favorite sauce. Yield: 24 ravioli.

Ravioli may be frozen on baking sheet and placed in plastic bag to be kept in freezer up to 3 months. Cook frozen ravioli for 3 minutes or just until tender.

BAY POINT CHILI-RUBBED GROUPER

1	tablespoon chili powder
2	teaspoons dillseeds
1	teaspoon lemon pepper
½	teaspoon ground cumin
¼	teaspoon thyme
4	(4 to 6-ounce) grouper filets
¼	cup butter or margarine

Garnishes: fresh thyme sprigs, lemon zest

Combine the chili powder, dillseeds, lemon pepper, cumin and thyme; press evenly over fillets.

Melt butter in a large skillet over medium heat; add fillets and cook 5 minutes on each side or until fish flakes easily with a fork. Garnish, if desired. Serve with lemon wedges. Yield: 4 servings.

BEER-BATTERED FLOUNDER FILLETS

2	pounds flounder fillets
1	fresh lemon, divided
1	teaspoon salt
1	cup all-purpose flour
1	can beer
2	tablespoons water
	dash paprika
	cooking oil for deep frying

Sprinkle fillets with juice of ½ lemon and ½ salt. Combine remaining salt and flour. Add beer and water to dry ingredients. Beat gradually, until batter is smooth. Dip fish in batter; drain slightly and fry in deep hot cooking oil, 350 degrees about 3 or 4 minutes. Fish should brown and flake easily when tested with fork. Drain on paper towels. Sprinkle with paprika and serve with tarter or cocktail sauce. Serves 4.

BLACKENED REDFISH

1	teaspoon paprika
½	teaspoon dried sage
½	teaspoon ground cumin
½	teaspoon garlic powder
½	teaspoon granulated sugar
½	teaspoon salt
¼	teaspoon ground red pepper (cayenne)
¼	teaspoon onion powder
4	redfish or farm-raised catfish fillets
	non-stick cooking spray
1	teaspoon olive oil
	lemon slices

Put paprika, sage, cumin, garlic powder, sugar, salt, red pepper and onion powder in a 1-gallon food storage bag. Close bag and shake until well blended.

Put 1 fillet in bag at a time and shake until lightly coated.

Coat large non-stick skillet with cooking spray. Add oil and heat over medium-low heat until hot. Add fillets, skinned side up and cook 4-5 minutes until lightly blackened. Carefully turn with spatula and cook 4 to 5 minutes longer, or until fish feels firm and is opaque at the thickest part. Serve with lemon slices. Yield: 4 servings.

Because fish are delicate and tender, avoid overcooking, which makes fish dry and tough. Cook until fish flakes easily with a fork. For food safety reasons, you should cook fish to an internal temperature of 160 degrees.

BODIE ISLAND BARBECUED BLUEFISH

½ cup fresh lime juice
¼ cup cider vinegar
4 cloves garlic, crushed
½ cup olive oil
2 teaspoons minced fresh ginger
salt and pepper to taste
bluefish fillets for six servings
lime slices for garnish

To prepare marinade combine lime juice, vinegar, garlic, olive oil, ginger, salt and pepper; whisk together to blend well. Set aside.

Rinse fillets, and cut out the dark vein of meat that runs down the fish fillet. Place fish in a shallow dish; pour marinade over fillets. Turn to coat both sides well, cover and refrigerate at least 3 hours. (I always marinate bluefish overnite).

When ready to cook, prepare coals or gas grill. Remove fish from marinade and reserve. Cook fish 10-12 minutes, turning once and brushing occasionally with reserve marinade. Fish will look lightly browned when done. Serve immediately with lime slices for garnish. Yield: 6 servings.

CAPE FEAR COCONUT SHRIMP WITH APRICOT SAUCE

1   pound jumbo shrimp, cleaned
1   cup blanched, whole almonds
1   bag (7 ounce) flaked coconut
½   cup all-purpose flour
2   eggs, lightly beaten
¼   teaspoon salt
    vegetable oil for frying

Apricot sauce as follows:
½   cup bottled duck sauce
½   cup apricot jam
½   teaspoon soy sauce

Butterfly shrimp; place cleaned shrimp on a cutting board and butter-fly-slice from the back outer edge. Do not cut all the way through.

Place almonds in a food processor or coffee grinder and process. Mix almonds, coconut and flour in a shallow bowl. Mix eggs and salt together. Dip each shrimp in egg, then coconut mixture.

Heat oil to 375 degrees. Fry 5 shrimp at a time, cooking a minute or two just until golden brown; remove and drain on paper towels.

Prepare the apricot sauce by mixing the duck sauce, apricot jam and soy sauce together. Serve shrimp with sauce. Yield: 8 servings.

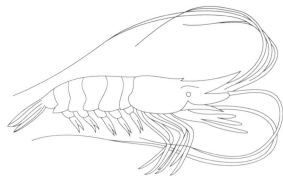

CAPE ROMAIN SCALLOPED OYSTERS

1	pound fresh oysters, shucked
½	cup butter or margarine, melted
¼	cup sliced celery
2	tablespoons minced onion
2	garlic cloves, minced
2	cups cracker crumbs
¾	cup milk
1	tablespoon minced parsley
1	teaspoon lemon juice
1	teaspoon salt
⅛	teaspoon pepper
½	cup grated Cheddar cheese

Pick through oysters to remove any remaining shell particles. Simmer oysters in their liquor until edges begin to curl. Remove from heat; drain. In a 10-inch frypan, heat butter or margarine over medium heat and saute celery, onion and garlic until tender. Add cracker crumbs, (reserving ½ cup), milk, parsley, lemon juice, salt and pepper, blending gently; add oysters.

Pour mixture into a well-greased, 1-quart, shallow baking dish. Combine reserved cracker crumbs and cheese. Sprinkle this mixture over casserole. Bake at 350 degrees , 15 to 20 minutes or until light golden brown. Yield: 4 servings.

Try these coating ideas for fish or shellfish when frying or baking:
Seasoned bread crumbs
Bread crumbs and Parmesan cheese
Bread crumbs and dry salad dressing mix
Cornmeal and chile powder [or Cajun spice]
Crushed cornflakes or other cereal
Crushed corn or potato chips

CAPERS ISLAND MACKEREL WITH MUSTARD

2 tablespoons dijon mustard
¼ cup finely chopped fresh cilantro
2 garlic cloves, finely crushed
2 teaspoons lemon juice
   salt and pepper
4 mackerel, about 10-ounces each
   rolled oats
   lemon wedges and cilantro sprigs for garnish

Preheat broiler. In a bowl, mix together mustard, cilantro, garlic and lemon juice. Season with salt and pepper.

Using the point of a very sharp knife, cut 3 slashes on each side of each mackerel. Spoon mustard mixture into slashes and sprinkle with oats. Wrap each fish in a large piece of foil and fold edges of foil together to seal tightly. Place foil packages under hot broiler 5 minutes. Open foil, turn fish, reseal foil and broil 2 to 3 minutes more. Open foil, place fish under broiler and broil 2 to 3 minutes or until cooked through and flesh flakes easily. Serve garnished with lemon wedges and cilantro sprigs. Yield: 4 servings.

CAPTAIN'S SEAFOOD FETTUCCINE ALFREDO

1	pound fresh lump crabmeat
¾	cup butter or margarine, divided
½	pound small scallops
½	pound shrimp, peeled and cleaned
3	cloves garlic, minced
1	pint half-and-half
1	(12-ounce) package fettuccini, cooked
½	cup grated Parmesan cheese
¼	cup chopped fresh parsley
½	teaspoon freshly ground pepper

Pick through crabmeat and remove any bits of shell; set aside. Melt 2 tablespoons of butter in a large skillet over medium heat. Saute scallops 1-2 minutes; add shrimp and saute 3 more minutes or until shrimp are pink. Remove seafood from skillet and keep warm.

In same skillet, melt remaining butter over medium heat; add pressed garlic, and saute until tender. Stir in half-and-half and bring to the boiling point. Reduce heat, and simmer, stirring occasionally, 5 to 7 minutes or until mixture is thickened.

Add crabmeat, shrimp, scallops and hot cooked pasta; warming through. Stir gently to blend; add Parmesan cheese, chopped parsley and pepper. Toss gently and serve immediately. Yield: 6 servings.

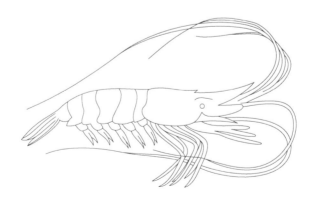

CAROLINA CRAB CAKES

1	pound fresh lump crabmeat
1	large egg
2	tablespoons mayonnaise
1	tablespoon lemon juice
2	teaspoons dijon mustard
1	teaspoon Old Bay seafood seasoning
1	teaspoon Worcestershire sauce
¼	cup red bell pepper, finely chopped
¼	cup green onions, finely chopped
¼	cup fresh parsley, chopped
1	cup fresh fine bread crumbs
	canola oil for frying
	lemon wedges for garnish

Carefully pick all shell material out of crab meat and set aside. In a large bowl, place egg, mayonnaise, lemon juice and dijon mustard. Using a wire whisk, blend all ingredients together. Add seafood seasoning, Worcestershire sauce, red bell pepper, green onion and parsley; blend together once more. Add crab and half of the bread crumbs. Turn gently to blend, being careful not to break up large lumps of crab. Add remaining bread crumbs in same gentle manner until crab mixture is easy enough to handle, yet loose. Form crab mixture into cakes ¾-inch thick, 3-inches in diameter. Saute in hot oil. Serve with tartar sauce and lemon wedges. Yield: 4 servings.

CHARCOAL GRILLED YELLOWFIN TUNA STEAKS

2	pounds yellowfin tuna steaks
¼	cup vegetable oil
¼	cup lemon juice
2	teaspoons salt
½	teaspoon Worcestershire sauce
¼	teaspoon white pepper
⅛	teaspoon liquid hot pepper sauce
	paprika

Cut steaks into serving-size portions and place in a well-greased, hinged wire grill. Combine vegetable oil, lemon juice, salt, Worcestershire sauce, white pepper and hot sauce; whisk together to blend. Baste fish with sauce and sprinkle with paprika. Cook about 4-inches from moderately hot coals for 5 to 6 minutes. Turn, baste with sauce and sprinkle with paprika; cook 4 to 5 minutes longer or until tuna has a slightly pink center. Yield: 6 servings.

COD BAKED IN PARCHMENT

	parchment paper (or aluminum foil)
2	tablespoons vegetable oil
2	pounds cod, cut into 6 steaks
12	scallions, chopped
2	tomatoes, chopped
1	zucchini, thinly sliced
	salt and pepper
1	teaspoon dried oregano
	juice of 2 lemons
2	tablespoons Parmesan cheese

Pre-heat oven to 375 degrees. Cut 6 pieces of parchment paper (or aluminum foil) into pieces large enough to enclose each fish steak and brush the pieces with oil. Place the fish in the center of each sheet and top with scallions, tomatoes and zucchini. Sprinkle with salt and pepper, oregano and some of the lemon juice. Top all off with Parmesan cheese and seal the package to completely enclose the fish. Place packages in a single layer on a cookie sheet and bake for 20 minutes. Fish may be served in its package. Yield: 6 servings.

CRAB MEAT NORFOLK

1   pound backfin lump crabmeat, picked
2   tablespoons butter, melted
    desired amount of fresh lemon juice
    salt and pepper to taste
2   tablespoons minced parsley
    paprika
    drizzle of dry white wine (optional)

Using 4 individual ovenproof casserole servers, divide crab meat equally and place in each dish. Pour over these the melted butter and fresh lemon juice. Season with salt and pepper to taste. Bake in a preheated 350 degrees oven until tops are slightly brown. Remove from oven and sprinkle with parsley and a light dash of paprika. A nice touch is to drizzle a small amount of white wine along the sides of each dish. It will bubble and sizzle to a tantalizing aroma. Serve immediately. Serves 4.

HOT CRAB MELT ON A BUN

1   can (6½-ounce) crab meat, drained and flaked
½   cup prepared tartar sauce
1   tablespoon celery, finely chopped
2   tablespoons green pepper, finely chopped
1   teaspoon lemon juice
2   English muffins, split and toasted
4   slices American Cheddar cheese

Preheat oven to 350 degrees. In a medium bowl, combine crabmeat, sauce, celery, green pepper and lemon juice. Spread equal amounts on muffin halves. Bake 5 minutes. Top each with a cheese slice; bake 5 minutes longer or until hot and bubbly. Serve immediately. Makes 4 servings.

CRAB-STUFFED SOFT-SHELL CRABS

12	soft-shell crabs, cleaned
¼	cup butter, melted
½	cup mayonnaise
1	tablespoon prepared mustard
1	tablespoon horseradish
1	teaspoon Old Bay seafood seasoning
1	teaspoon Worcestershire sauce
1	tablespoon fresh lemon juice
1	small red hot chili pepper, diced (optional)
½	cup onion, diced
¼	cup fresh parsley, chopped
	salt to taste
1	pound backfin crabmeat
½	cup breadcrumbs (or more)

To do ahead: Pre-heat oven to broil. Place soft-shell crabs in a baking pan. Brush each side with melted butter. Broil crabs 2 to 3 minutes on each side or until color changes to red. Remove from oven and set aside.

Crab stuffing: In a large bowl, mix mayonnaise, mustard and horserad-ish. Add seafood seasoning, Worcestershire and lemon juice. Turn in chili pepper (if desired), onion and parsley. Salt to taste. Gently fold in crabmeat so as not to break up chunks, with enough breadcrumbs to form a man-ageable crab mixture to handle for stuffing.

To assemble: Gently lift the two sides of each crab shell and insert crabmeat stuffing to hold. When all of the soft-shell crabs are stuffed, a dollop of remaining crabmeat stuffing can be placed on top of each crab. Bake in a preheated 350 degree oven for 10 to 15 minutes or until done. Serves 6.

Note: These crabs go marvelously served with our linguini and fresh clam sauce.

DEVILISH DEVILED CRABS

2	cups softened bread crumbs (4 slices bread)
½	cup milk
4	cups flaked crabmeat
½	cup margarine or butter, melted
1	teaspoon dry mustard
¼	teaspoon ground red pepper
2	eggs, beaten
2	green onions, chopped
12	crab shells (scallop shells or ramekins)

Heat oven to 400 degrees. Grease the crab shells (or ramekins). Mix bread crumbs and milk in large bowl. Mix in crabmeat, butter or margarine, mustard, red pepper, eggs and green onion and gently blend. Spoon crab mixture into greased shells and place in baking pan. Bake 20 to 25 minutes or until lightly browned. Yield: 6 servings (2 crabs each).

FISH IN SPICY SAUCE

2 tablespoons butter or margarine
2 teaspoons hot chili powder
2 medium size Spanish onions, finely chopped
1 garlic clove, peeled and crushed
2 cups chicken stock
2 tablespoons tomato paste
1 lemon, juice extracted
1 pound firm white fish (grouper or dolphin), cut into chunks
    salt and freshly ground black pepper
    cooked white rice

Melt the butter in a large saucepan over low heat; add the chili powder and cook for about 2 minutes. Add the onions and garlic and cook for 3 to 5 minutes. Add the chicken stock, tomato paste and lemon juice. Cover pan and simmer on low heat for about 30 minutes, until sauce is thick and creamy. Place the chunks of fish directly into the sauce being sure to cover the fish with the sauce. Season with salt and pepper to taste. Cover and simmer for 10 minutes. Remove from heat, and serve over rice.

Yield: 4 servings.

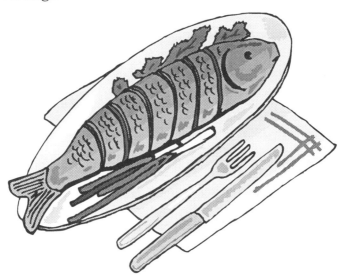

FOLLY BEACH OVEN-FRIED FISH

¼   cup cornmeal
¼   cup fine, dry breadcrumbs
½   teaspoon salt
½   teaspoon paprika
½   teaspoon dillweed
⅛   teaspoon pepper
1   pound fish fillets, cut into 1-inch strips (grouper, halibut, trout)
⅓   cup milk
3   tablespoons butter or margarine, melted
     lemon slices

Combine cornmeal, breadcrumbs, salt, paprika, dillweed and pepper in a shallow dish. Dip fish in milk, and dredge in cornmeal mixture. Place in a lightly greased 13x9x2-inch pan, and drizzle with butter. Bake at 450 degrees for 10 minutes or until fish flakes easily when tested with a fork. Garnish with lemon slices. Yield: 4-6 servings.

FRIED CATFISH, SPOT OR CROAKER
FROM KITTY HAWK

1   pound catfish, spot or croaker fillets
     salt and pepper to taste
½   cup flour
1   cup cornmeal
½   teaspoon paprika
2   eggs, slightly beaten
1   tablespoon water
     oil for frying

Sprinkle fillets with salt and pepper. Place flour and cornmeal in two shallow bowls. Dredge each fillet in flour, then dip in beaten eggs, then in cornmeal. Refrigerate fish for 30 minutes. When ready to cook, remove fish fillets from refrigerator and heat oil in a heavy skillet, over medium heat. Fry fish 3 minutes on each side, or until fish flakes when touched with a fork. Yield: 4 servings

GRILLED SEAFOOD KABOBS

Marinade:
½   cup olive oil
3   tablespoons lemon juice
1   tablespoon fresh parsley, chopped
1   tablespoon fresh basil, chopped
1   tablespoon capers, drained
1   green onion, chopped
     salt and freshly ground pepper
Kabobs:
4   ounces monkfish
4   ounces rockfish
12   medium raw shrimp in shells
12   large scallops
8   large mushroom caps
1   large red bell pepper, cut into 2-inch pieces
1   yellow onion, cut into 8 wedges
8   firm cherry tomatoes
8   bay leaves
     Favorite rice recipe, prepared for 4

Prepare marinade by placing oil, lemon juice, parsley, basil, capers, green onion, salt and pepper in a food processor or blender; processing until smooth. Reserve.

Cut fish into 1-inch cubes. Alternate fish, shrimp, scallops, vegetables and bay leaves on each of four 12-inch metal skewers. Place kabobs on ungreased rectangular baking dish 13x9x2 inches. Drizzle marinade over kabobs. Cover and refrigerate at least 45 minutes.

When ready to cook, remove kabobs from marinade; reserve marinade. Grill kabobs uncovered about 4 inches from hot coals 10 minutes, turning once and brushing with reserved marinade occasionally, until fish flakes easily with fork. Discard bay leaves. Serve kabobs over your favorite prepared rice recipe. Yield: 4 servings.

LOW-COUNTRY SHRIMP AND GRITS

1	recipe (6 servings) stone ground grits
¾	cup grated sharp Cheddar cheese
	Tabasco sauce
	freshly grated nutmeg
	white pepper
6	strips bacon, diced
4	tablespoons unsalted butter
1	cup yellow onion, chopped
½	pound fresh mushroom, sliced
2	cloves garlic, minced
3	cups fresh chopped tomatoes
2	teaspoons Worcestershire sauce
	dash hot sauce
1	pound shrimp, peeled and cleaned
	salt and pepper to taste

Prepare the grits according to the directions using the full amount of cheese. Season to taste, but lightly, with tabasco, nutmeg, and white pepper. Keep warm.

Saute the bacon in a Dutch oven. When almost crisp, remove bacon and reserve as a garnish. Add the butter to the skillet and saute the onions and mushrooms till tender, about 4-6 minutes. Add the garlic; saute one minute more. Add the tomatoes, Worcestershire and hot sauce. Simmer 10 minutes to cook the tomatoes and blend the flavors. Add the shrimp and cook until they turn pink and curl. The size of the shrimp will determine this cooking time. Season with salt and pepper to taste, garnish with cooked bacon and serve over hot grits. Yield: 6 servings.

OCEAN SANDS SEA TROUT

6   skinless sea trout fillets
3   tablespoons flour
½   cup milk
3   cups salted potato chips, crushed
½   cup vegetable oil
2   tablespoons butter
     tartar sauce and lemon wedges
     freshly ground pepper

Place the flour in a shallow bowl, and do the same with the milk and the crushed potato chips. Dredge the fish fillets in flour, then milk, then the chips.

In a large skillet, heat the vegetable oil and butter together over medium-high heat. Brown the fillets on each side and remove to a baking dish. Bake sea trout in a pre-heated 350 degrees oven for 5 minutes or until fillets are cooked. Serve with tartar sauce and lemon wedges. Yield: 5 servings.

OREGON INLET SHRIMP WITH FETA AND OREGANO

1   tablespoon extra-virgin olive oil
3   cloves garlic, chopped
1   pound medium shrimp, peeled
2   tablespoons fresh lemon juice
¼   cup fresh oregano leaves, chopped
⅛   teaspoon salt
2   ounces feta cheese, crumbled

Heat oil in skillet. Add garlic and cook 1 minute. Add shrimp and cook 2 minutes. Turn shrimp over and cook 1 minute longer. Add lemon juice and oregano and cook 1 minute. Remove skillet from heat.

Add salt and feta cheese to pan and toss. (Feta will melt and become creamy, with some small chunks remaining). Serve immediately. Serves 4.

OVEN-BAKED CLAMS COROLLA

12	large fresh clams
½	cup frozen chopped spinach, defrosted and drained
1	cup fresh breadcrumbs
¼	cup fresh parsley, chopped
2	tablespoons Parmesan cheese
2	large garlic cloves, minced
	salt and pepper to taste
2	tablespoons butter, melted
	olive oil for drizzling
	lemon wedges for garnish

Using a vegetable brush, scrub the clams clean. Place cleaned clams in a bowl of ice-water to make opening them easier. Open each clam, reserving the natural juices. Place the half shells containing the clams on an oven-proof dish. Place a scant teaspoonful of spinach around each clam.

In a medium bowl, mix breadcrumbs, parsley, cheese, garlic, salt, pepper and melted butter together with a fork. Sprinkle each clam with breadcrumb mixture and a drizzle of olive oil over all. Bake in a 400 degree oven for 10 minutes. Garnish with lemon and serve immediately.

Make sandwich spreads with drained canned seafood (shrimp, crab, clams, salmon, tuna). Mix with mayonnaise, onion, celery and a squirt of lemon juice.

OYSTER-CORNBREAD STUFFING

1	can (15 1/2 ounce) oysters, fresh or frozen
1	cup chopped celery
1	cup chopped onion
¼	cup butter or margarine, melted
3½	cups toasted cornbread cubes
½	cup chicken broth
1	teaspoon poultry seasoning
1	teaspoon sage

Thaw oysters if frozen. Drain oysters; remove any remaining shell particles. Saute celery and onion in butter until tender; add oysters. Cook 3 to 5 minutes or until edges of oysters begin to curl. Combine cornbread, chicken broth, poultry seasoning and sage in a mixing bowl. Add oysters, celery and onions, blending gently. Makes 4 cups of stuffing, enough to stuff a 4-pound bird.

PAN-FRIED SOFT-SHELL BLUE CRABS

12	soft-shell blue crabs, medium size, cleaned
2	eggs, beaten
¼	cup milk
2	teaspoons salt
¾	cup flour
¾	cup dry bread crumbs
	blend of butter or margarine & vegetable oil for frying

Combine egg, milk and salt. Dip cleaned and dry crabs in egg mixture. Combine flour and crumbs. Dip crabs in flour and crumb mixture. Fry in butter-vegetable oil blend until golden. Serves 6.

RED SNAPPER VERACRUZ

2	pounds red snapper fillets
2	limes
5	tablespoons olive oil
½	cup chopped onion
3	cloves garlic
3	large tomatoes, peeled and chopped
10	pitted green olives, chopped
2	tablespoon capers
2	bay leaves
2	jalapeno peppers, seeded and sliced
½	teaspoon salt
¼	teaspoon freshly ground pepper
1	tablespoon chopped fresh cilantro
	lime slices

Preheat the oven to 325 degrees. Squeeze lime juice over the fish and set aside until ready to cook.

Saute onion and garlic in oil until soft. Stir in tomatoes, olives, capers, bay leaves, jalapenos, salt and pepper. Bring to a boil, then reduce heat and simmer, uncovered, 10 minutes.

Place fish in a large skillet and sprinkle with salt. Pour tomato mixture over fish. Bring to a boil, reduce heat, cover and simmer about 7 minutes or until fish turns from translucent to opaque. Discard bay leaves. Garnish with lime slices and cilantro. Serve over rice. Serves 6 to 8.

Fish may be purchased fresh, frozen and canned. For the best quality in taste, texture and nutrition, always try to buy fresh fish.

ROASTED OYSTERS, WANCHESE-STYLE

24   oysters, scrubbed
¼   cup clarified butter
¼   cup seafood cocktail sauce
½   lemon, cut into wedges

Prepare and heat grill. Spread the oysters on a grill rack and place the rack over the grill about 6 inches above the heat source. If the oysters don't fit on the rack, cook them in batches. Cook oysters until the shells are hot and you see them pop open slightly. Immediately remove them from the grill, pile them in a bucket or on a deep-rimmed platter, and serve them at once with the butter, cocktail sauce and lemon wedges. For each person, allow 12 to 24 oysters.

SALMON STEAKS WITH LEMON-MUSTARD SAUCE

3   tablespoons dry white wine
2   tablespoons fresh lemon juice
2   tablespoons reduced-fat mayonnaise
2   teaspoons dijon mustard
1   teaspoon paprika
¼   teaspoon garlic powder
1   teaspoon pepper
4   (4 to 6-ounce) salmon steaks

In a small bowl, whisk together wine, lemon juice, mayonnaise, mustard, paprika and garlic powder; cover and chill.

Sprinkle pepper over both sides of each salmon steak. Coat a food rack with cooking spray; place on grill over high heat (400 degrees - 500 degrees). Place salmon on rack, and cook, covered with grill lid, 3 to 4 minutes on each side or until fish flakes easily with a fork. Spoon sauce over fish; serve with lemon wedges. Yield: 4 servings.

SAUTEED SHRIMP WITH SPINACH AND POLENTA

½   cup extra-virgin olive oil, divided
4   cloves garlic, sliced thin and divided
½   pound fresh spinach, stems removed and leaves torn into small pieces
3   tablespoons fresh lemon juice, divided
¼   teaspoon salt
¼   teaspoon freshly ground pepper
    pinch of sugar
1   pound large shrimp, shelled and deveined
⅓   cup dry white wine
1   tablespoon fresh parsley, finely chopped
    Prepared recipe for Herbed Polenta (recipe follows)

Heat 4 tablespoons of olive oil in a large skillet over medium heat. Add 2 thinly sliced cloves of garlic and cook over low heat, stirring often until garlic is golden. Add spinach to the oil mixture; increase heat to medium and cook, stirring constantly for about 3 minutes or until spinach is limp. Stir in 1 tablespoon lemon juice, salt, pepper, and sugar.

Heat remaining 4 tablespoons of oil and 2 cloves of garlic in a large skillet over medium heat. Add shrimp and cook, stirring often, for 3 to 5 minutes or until shrimp turn pink. Add remaining 2 tablespoons of lemon juice, wine and parsley. Bring to a boil, cook for about 30 seconds. Season to taste with salt and pepper. Serve immediately with spinach and polenta, pouring the pan juices over the shrimp. Yield: 4 servings.

Herbed Polenta: In a heavy saucepan, bring 3 cups canned low-sodium chicken broth and 1 tablespoon olive oil to a boil over medium-high heat. Gradually, whisk in 1 cup yellow cornmeal, stirring constantly. Reduce heat to low and simmer, whisking often, for 10 minutes or until polenta is thick. Remove from heat and stir in 2 tablespoons fresh grated Parmesan cheese, and 1 tablespoon each of finely chopped fresh parsley and basil.

SEA BREEZE MAHI-MAHI ALMONDINE

4	mahi-mahi fillets (8 ounces each)
	flour seasoned to taste with salt and pepper
¼	cup olive oil
1	cup Chablis
½	cup sliced, toasted almonds
1	tablespoon finely chopped parsley
2	tablespoons fresh lemon juice
2	tablespoons capers
3	drops Tabasco sauce
1	stick butter
	toasted almond slices for garnish (optional)

Cut fish fillets into 8-ounce serving size pieces and set aside. Prepare seasoned flour and place in a flat bowl. Heat olive oil in skillet. Dredge fish in seasoned flour and shake off excess. Put fillets in heated oil and saute until golden brown on each side.

Remove fillets from skillet and set aside.

Discard any remaining olive oil in skillet. Deglaze pan with wine. Stir in almonds, parsley, lemon juice, capers and hot sauce.

Add butter. Stir until butter is melted and the sauce thickens.

Serve warm fish fillets topped with almond-caper sauce. Garnish with additional toasted almond slices, if desired. Serves 4.

When selecting fresh fish, always look for the following:
Eyes should be bright, clear not sunken.
Gills should be reddish-pink, never brown.
Flesh should be firm and elastic.
There should be no objectionable odor.

SEAFOOD ENCHILADAS WITH SPICY GREEN SAUCE

1	(7-ounce) jar green taco sauce
⅓	cup dairy sour cream
1	(8-ounce) package cream cheese or 1½ cups cottage cheese
2	tablespoons milk
1	clove garlic, minced
¼	teaspoon salt
⅓	cup green onions, sliced
8	7-inch flour tortillas
8	ounces Monterey Jack cheese, shredded
1½	cups desired cooked seafood such as shrimp or crab
2	tablespoons grated Parmesan cheese
	chopped ripe olives

In a small mixing bowl, combine taco sauce and sour cream; set aside. In a blender container or food processor bowl, combine cream or cottage cheese, milk, garlic, and salt. Cover and blend or process till mixture is smooth. Set aside. Reserve 1 tablespoon of the green onion. Spread 1 tablespoon of the taco sauce mixture over each tortilla. Top each with shredded cheese, seafood, and remaining green onion.

Spoon remaining taco sauce mixture into the bottom of a greased 12x7 ½x2-inch baking dish. Roll up tortillas and place, seam side down, in baking dish. Pour cheese mixture over tortillas; sprinkle with Parmesan. Bake, uncovered, in a 350 degree oven for 25 to 30 minutes or till heated through. Before serving, sprinkle with reserved green onion and olives. Makes 8 servings.

SEARED SCALLOPS WITH TOMATO-MANGO SALSA

1	medium tomato, finely chopped
¾	cup finely chopped mango
3	tablespoons finely chopped purple onion
2	tablespoons finely chopped fresh basil
2	tablespoons red wine vinegar
1	tablespoon capers
1	tablespoon olive oil
12	sea scallops
¼	teaspoon salt
¼	teaspoon pepper
¼	avocado, sliced

Garnish: fresh basil sprigs

Combine tomato, mango, purple onion, basil, vinegar and capers. Cover and refrigerate at least 30 minutes.

Heat olive oil in a skillet over medium heat until hot. Add scallops, and cook 3 minutes or until done, turning once. Remove scallops from skillet; sprinkle with salt and pepper. Arrange scallops, salsa, and avocado slices evenly on plates. Garnish with basil and serve. Yield: 2 servings.

SHRIMP WITH CORNCAKES AND BLACK BEAN SALSA

2   naval oranges, peeled and cleaned
1   tablespoon fresh lime juice
1   can (15 ounce) black beans, rinsed
1   avocado, peeled and cut into 1/2" chunks
½   cup chopped cilantro
1   jalapeno pepper, seeded and minced
     non-stick cooking spray
1½ pounds large shrimp, peeled and deveined
¼   teaspoon each salt and pepper
     Corncake recipe in bread section of this book

Section oranges and cut into small chunks. Squeeze juice from membranes into a medium bowl. Add oranges and stir in lime juice, black beans, avocado, cilantro and jalapeno pepper. Cover bowl, and refrigerate at least 2 hours, for flavors to blend.

About 25 minutes before serving, prepare corncakes.

Heat broiler or grill pan. Lightly coat shrimp with non-stick spray, then sprinkle with salt and pepper. Broil 4 to 6 inches from heat source or cook in grill pan 2 to 3 minutes per side until shrimp are just barely opaque at center. Serve with salsa and corncakes. Serves 6.

Grilling baskets make turning delicate fish a breeze. Spray insides of basket with Vegetable cooking spray first, then proceed to grill.

SHRIMP WITH LINGUINE AND PESTO

8   ounces linguine
½   cup prepared pesto
1   teaspoon olive oil
3   cloves garlic, minced
1   pound medium shrimp, peeled
1   pint cherry tomatoes, cut in half
⅛   teaspoon salt
¼   cup Parmesan cheese

Cook linguine in boiling salted water according to package directions. Drain. Toss linguine with pesto.

Meanwhile, heat oil in skillet. Add garlic and cook, stirring, 1 minute. Add shrimp and cook 2 minutes. Turn shrimp over and cook 2 minutes longer. Toss pasta and shrimp with tomatoes, salt and cheese. Serve immediately. Makes 4 servings.

Raw shrimp (heads removed) are greenish or pink and are sold frozen or refrigerated by the pound. One and a half pounds of raw shrimp will yield ¾ pound cooked (about 2 cups). Cooked shrimp (shells removed) are pink and are sold by the pound. Canned shrimp can be used interchangeably with cooked shrimp.

SOUTH ISLAND LEMON-LIME MONKFISH

	juice of 1 lemon
	juice of 1 lime
½	cup olive oil
3	cloves garlic, minced
½	tablespoon fresh basil, chopped
	salt and freshly ground pepper to taste
1	pound monkfish, skinned and trimmed
	lemon and lime slices for garnish

To prepare marinade, combine lemon and lime juices with olive oil, stirring constantly until well blended. Add garlic, basil, salt and pepper. Set aside.

Place fish in a shallow glass dish. Pour marinade over fish; cover and refrigerate for at least 1 hour.

When ready to cook, remove fish from marinade and place in a grilling basket. Grill over hot coals, about 5 minutes. Turn fish, brush with marinade and cook 2-3 minutes more with grill top closed. Fish should flake easily when touched with a fork. Garnish with lemon and lime slices and serve immediately. Yield: 4 servings.

SOUTHERN SHORES SEA BASS AND GARLIC

1½	tablespoons unsalted butter
8	garlic cloves, lightly crushed
16	green onions, sliced
4	sea bass fillets with skin
	salt and pepper
2	slices lean smoked slab bacon, cut into thin strips
1	sprig thyme
½	cup fish stock or chicken broth
1	tablespoon chopped fresh parsley
	tarragon sprigs to garnish
	boiled new potatoes to serve

Melt butter in a heavy, shallow flameproof pan. Add garlic and green onions and cook over low heat until browned. Season skin side of fish, then add to casserole skin side down, with bacon and thyme. In a 400 degree pre-heated oven, cook about 20 minutes, then turn fish over and add stock. Bake 4 to 6 minutes until fish flakes. Discard thyme. Stir in parsley, and add seasoning, if necessary. Garnish with sprigs of tarragon and serve with new potatoes. Yield: 4 servings.

ST. HELENA SHRIMP SCAMPI

1   tablespoon butter
2   tablespoons olive oil
4   cloves garlic, finely chopped
1   pound large or medium-size shrimp, peeled and cleaned
¼   cup dry white wine
1   tablespoon fresh lemon juice
½   teaspoon salt
⅛   teaspoon pepper
1   tablespoon flavored bread crumbs
2   tablespoons fresh parsley

Heat butter and oil in large skillet over high heat. When butter starts to brown, add garlic. Reduce heat; cook 1 minute, stirring to prevent garlic from over browning.

Add shrimp; cook 2 minutes, stirring once. Add wine, lemon juice, salt and pepper; cook 2 minutes or until shrimp are cooked through. Stir in bread crumbs and parsley. Serve immediately. Yield: 4 servings.

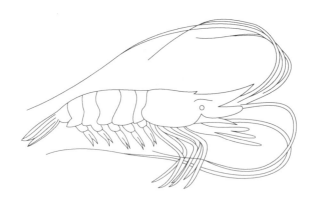

STEAMER POT SEAFOOD FEAST

½   cup Old Bay Seasoning
     water and beer
3   pounds seafood (crabs, shrimp, clams, and mussels)
4   ears fresh corn in the husk
     new potatoes
1   tablespoon parsley flakes
     melted butter (optional)

In a large steamer pot with a raised rack at least 2 inches high, add equal amounts of beer and water to just below level of steamer rack. Layer potatoes crabs and corn, sprinkling the crabs with the seafood seasoning. Cover and steam approximately 35 minutes. During the last 15 minutes of cooking, add additional layers of seafood; shrimp, clams and mussels. Sprinkle each layer with seasoning. Steam crabs until red, shrimp until pink and clams and mussels until they open. Discard any that do not open. Garnish with parsley and serve with melted butter if desired. Makes 4 servings.

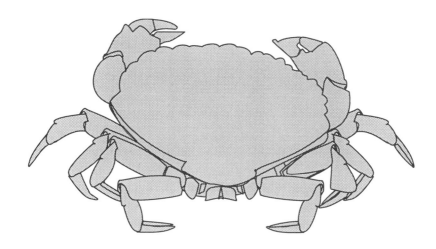

SWASH INLET SHRIMP AND SCALLOPS

3	tablespoons butter
2	tablespoons garlic, chopped
½	pound sea scallops
¼	cup parsley, chopped
	salt and pepper to taste
⅓	cup sun-dried tomatoes, julienned
¼	cup chardonnay
1	pound jumbo shrimp, shelled and deveined
¾	cup heavy cream (more if desired)
8	ounces cooked fettuccine

In a saucepan over medium heat, melt butter; stir in chopped garlic and saute briefly until garlic begins to pale. Stir in scallops, parsley, salt and pepper, tomatoes and wine. Saute 3 to 4 minutes, stirring, until scallops are tender and wine reduced.

Add shrimp and heavy cream, continue cooking about 2 minutes more, until shrimp are pink and cream begins to thicken. Add more cream if desired Serve over cooked fettuccine. Serves 4.

SWORDFISH GRILLED IN ORIENTAL SHERRY SAUCE

½	cup soy sauce
½	cup dry cooking sherry
1	tablespoon lemon juice
¼	cup vegetable oil
2	cloves garlic, crushed
4	swordfish fillets

Prepare marinade by combining soy sauce, sherry, lemon juice, vegetable oil and garlic in a mixing bowl and whisking together. Pour over the fish fillets in a shallow glass bowl. Cover and refrigerate at least 2 hours.

When ready to cook, remove fish from marinade and place in a grilling basket, reserving marinade. Grill over hot coals for 8 to 10 minutes, turning once and brushing fish with marinade once or twice during cooking. Fish should flake when touched with a fork. Serve immediately. Yield: 4 servings.

THAI GRILLED SHRIMP FROM KILL DEVIL HILLS

Dipping sauce:
½   cup peanut butter
½   cup water
1   tablespoon brown sugar, packed
1   tablespoon lemon juice
½   teaspoon salt
½   teaspoon red pepper sauce

1   small clove garlic
2   tablespoons vegetable oil
2   tablespoons water
1   tablespoon lemon juice
1   tablespoon brown sugar, packed
½   teaspoon salt
¼   teaspoon red pepper sauce
1½   pounds large shrimp, peeled and deveined
2   lime wedges

Place peanut butter, water, brown sugar, lemon juice, salt and red pepper sauce in a food processor. Cover and process on medium speed about 20 seconds or until smooth. Cover and let stand until serving.

Mix garlic, vegetable oil, water, lemon juice, brown sugar, salt and red pepper sauce in a shallow nonmetal dish. Add shrimp, turning to coat and marinate, refrigerated about 30 minutes. Heat coals or gas grill. Remove shrimp from marinade and thread on skewers. Reserve marinade. Cover and grill shrimp 4 to 6 inches from medium heat 10 to 20 minutes; turning and brushing 2 or 3 times with marinade, until shrimp are pink and firm. Serve with sauce and lime wedges. Serves 4.

TIDEWATER BOW TIE PASTA WITH SHRIMP, SCALLOPS AND MUSSELS

1	whole, roasted, red pepper, chopped (recipe in vegetable section)
¾	pound bow tie pasta
12	large shrimp, (about ¾ pound)
12	sea scallops (about ½ pound)
12	mussels (about ¼ pound)
	salt and pepper for seasoning
¼	cup olive oil
6-8	garlic cloves
3	tablespoons minced shallot
1	quart fish stock (recipe this book)
1½	tablespoons fresh basil leaves, sliced thin
1½	tablespoons flat leaf parsley
	salt & pepper to taste

Prepare roasted red pepper if using recipe in this book. Set aside.

Start heating water for pasta. Shell and devein shrimp and season with salt and pepper. Pat scallops dry and do the same. Scrub mussels well, and remove beards. When pasta water boils, cook bow tie pasta according to directions.

While pasta cooks, heat oil in a heavy 12-inch skillet over medium high heat. Saute shrimp and scallops just until golden, but not cooked through, turning once; about two minutes total. Add garlic, shallots and mussels and saute one minute. Add stock and bring to a boil. Simmer, covered, stirring occasionally until mixture is reduced by about one third. Stir in pasta, basil, parsley and salt and pepper to taste. Serves 4.

TUNA WITH LEMON AND CAPERS

6   (¾-inch-thick) tuna steaks
½   teaspoon salt
½   teaspoon freshly ground pepper
½   cup olive oil
¼   cup lemon juice
½   cup chopped, fresh parsley
½   cup capers, drained and chopped

Sprinkle steaks with salt and pepper. Heat half of oil in a large heavy skillet over medium-high heat. Add 3 tuna steaks to skillet, and cook 2 to 3 minutes on each side, or until done. Remove from skillet and keep warm. Repeat procedure with remaining olive oil and tuna steaks. Sprinkle steaks evenly with lemon juice, chopped parsley, and chopped capers. Serve immediately. Yield: 6 servings.

Fish in each of the following groups may be substituted for one another in recipes. If one is out of season, try one of the following:
Flounder, sole, sea trout, ocean perch, pompano.
Red snapper, grouper, mahi-mahi, sea bass.
Cod, haddock, halibut, tilefish, whiting, monkfish.
Tuna, mackerel, swordfish, bonito, king fish.
Croaker, spot, shark, swordfish, weakfish.
Mussels, clams, oysters.
Shrimps, scallops, lobster.

Desserts

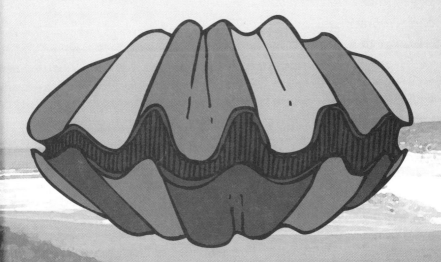

Desserts

ALBAMARLE APPLE CRISP

- ¾ cup corn flake crumbs
- ½ cup all-purpose flour
- ½ teaspoon salt
- ½ cup firmly packed brown sugar
- ⅓ cup chopped nuts
- ½ cup margarine or butter, softened
- 1 can apple pie filling (20 ounce)
- 1 tablespoon lemon juice
- 1 teaspoon ground cinnamon

Heat oven to 400 degrees. For topping mix, mix the corn flake crumbs, flour, salt, packed brown sugar, nuts and butter. Set aside.

In an ungreased 8x8x2 inch glass baking dish, stir the apple pie filling, lemon juice and cinnamon. Crumble topping evenly over apple mixture.

Bake about 30 minutes or until topping is crisp. Serve warm or cooled with ice cream or whipped topping. Serves 8.

CAPE LOOKOUT LEMON CLOUD PIE

1	package lemon pudding and pie filling
½	cup sugar
1¾	cups water
1	egg, slightly beaten
1½	cups thawed, nondairy whipped topping
½	cup shredded, sweetened coconut
1	prepared graham-cracker crust
	fresh lemon slices for garnish

Beat together the pudding mix, sugar, ¼ cup of the water and the egg in a medium-size saucepan. Mix in the remaining water until well blended. Place saucepan over medium heat and cook, stirring, until mixture comes to a full boil. Remove saucepan from heat, and let cool to room temperature, stirring occasionally.

When completely cooled, whisk lightly. Then fold in whipped topping and coconut until evenly mixed. Spread the filling evenly in the crumb crust. Top with lemon slices. Refrigerate until set, about 40 minutes. Serves 8.

CAT ISLAND CHOCOLATE TURTLE PIE

¼	cup caramel dessert topping
1	prepared graham cracker pie crust
½	cup chopped pecans
2	packages chocolate pudding and pie filling
3	cups milk
1	container whipped topping, thawed

Spread caramel topping on bottom of crust. Sprinkle with pecans, refrigerate. Stir pudding mixes into milk in medium saucepan. Stirring constantly, cook on medium heat until mixture comes to a full boil. Remove from heat. Cool 5 minutes, stirring twice. Pour into crust. Place plastic wrap on surface of filling.

Refrigerate 3 hours or until set. Garnish with whipped topping. Keep leftovers refrigerated. Yield: 8 servings.

CURRITUCK PEACH-BERRY COBBLER

1 cup all-purpose flour
½ cup granulated sugar
1½ teaspoons baking powder
½ cup milk
¼ cup butter, softened
¼ cup packed brown sugar
1 tablespoon cornstarch
½ cup cold water
3 cups fresh sliced peaches
1 cup fresh blueberries
1 tablespoon butter
1 tablespoon lemon juice
2 tablespoons coarse granulated sugar
¼ teaspoon ground nutmeg or cinnamon
   vanilla ice cream (optional)

NOTE: You may substitute frozen berries and canned peaches using ½ cup syrup in place of the cold water.

For topping, stir together flour, ½ cup granulated sugar, and baking powder. Add milk and ¼ cup butter. Stir till smooth; set aside.

For filling, in a medium saucepan stir together brown sugar and cornstarch; stir in water. Add peaches and blueberries. Cook and stir over medium heat till thickened and bubbly. Add 1 tablespoon butter and lemon juice; stir till butter melts. Pour into a 1½-quart ungreased casserole. Spoon topping in mounds over hot filling; spread evenly over filling. Sprinkle with a mixture of 2 tablespoons coarse sugar and nutmeg or cinnamon. Place on a shallow baking pan in oven.

Bake cobbler in a 350 degree oven about 35 minutes till bubbly and a toothpick inserted in middle comes out clean. Serve warm with ice cream if desired. Makes 6 servings.

KURE BEACH KEY LIME PIE

1   9-inch graham cracker crumb crust
2   (14-ounce) cans condensed milk
4   egg yolks, beaten
¾   cup lime juice
1   tablespoon grated lime peel
1   pint heavy cream, whipped
    mint leaves
8   lime slices

Mix condensed milk with egg yolks, lime juice and lime peel. Pour into piecrust. Bake 5 minutes in 300 degrees oven. Refrigerate for 1 hour. Cover with whipped cream; garnish with lime slices and mint leaves. Yield: 6 to 8 servings.

LOWLAND FRESH FRUIT CHEESECAKE

2   (8-ounce) packages of cream cheese, softened
½   cup sugar
½   teaspoon vanilla
2   eggs
1   prepared graham cracker crumb crust (9-inch)
2   cups sliced assorted fresh fruit

Mix cheese, sugar and vanilla with electric mixer on medium speed until well blended. Add eggs; mix until blended. Pour into crust. Bake at 350 degrees for 40 minutes or until center is almost set. Cool. Refrigerate 3 hours or overnight. Top with fruit before serving. Yield: 8 to 10 servings.

MACKEY'S FERRY PEANUT CHIFFON PIE

1	(8-ounce) package cream cheese, softened
1	(8-ounce) container cool whip, defrosted
½	cup peanut butter
½	cup confectioner's sugar
1	teaspoon vanilla
1	chocolate pie crust, prepared (recipe follows)

Mix cream cheese, cool whip, peanut butter and sugar together. Add vanilla. Pour mixture into chocolate pie crust and chill till firm.

COMPANION RECIPE
Chocolate Pie Crust

1½	cup chocolate wafer cookie crumbs
¼	cup butter, melted
⅓	cup sugar

Heat oven to 350 degrees. Mix crumbs, butter and sugar. If desired, reserve 2 to 3 tablespoons crumb mixture for topping. Press remaining mixture firmly and evenly against bottom and sides of 9-inch pie pan. Bake 10 minutes. Cool.

You can wrap a homemade unbaked pie crust and store it in the freezer for up to two months.

OLD SOUTHERN FRESH PEACH PIE

½ cup sugar
3 tablespoons all-purpose flour
½ teaspoon ground cinnamon
¼ teaspoon salt
6 large, ripe peaches, peeled and sliced
1 tablespoon lemon juice
¼ teaspoon almond extract
2 frozen pie crusts
   milk or water, sugar

Combine sugar, flour, cinnamon and salt in a small bowl. Put peaches in a large bowl: sprinkle with lemon juice and almond extract. Toss to coat; add sugar mixture; mix gently. Spoon peaches into thawed pie shell. Put other pie shell over the top of the pie and crimp sides together. Cut several vents in the pie shell for steam to escape. Brush pastry with milk or water; sprinkle with sugar.

Bake in a 425 degree oven for 15 minutes. Lower heat to 350 degrees; bake 35 minutes longer or until golden and juices are bubbly. Cool. Yield: 6 servings.

PEACH MELBA ICE CREAM PIE

1 prepared graham-cracker pie crust
2 pints vanilla ice cream
¾ cup peach preserves
½ cup seedless raspberry spread
½ pint raspberries
2 medium ripe peaches, sliced
3 tablespoons seedless raspberry spread
   mint sprigs for garnish

Put spoonfuls of ice cream into a large bowl. Add peach preserves and stir vigorously until blended. Spread half in crust. Place pie and bowl in freezer until ice cream in pie is firm, about 1 hour. Remove pie from freezer and spread pie with spreadable fruit; freeze 1 hour or until set. Remove bowl from freezer. Spread pie with remaining mixture in bowl. Freeze 4 hours until firm.

Fifteen minutes before serving, remove pie from freezer. Top with berries, peaches and spreadable fruit; garnish with mint leaves. Serves 10.

SOUTHERN PECAN PIE

     prepared 9" pie shell
3   eggs
⅔   cup sugar
½   teaspoon salt
⅓   cup butter or margarine, melted
1   cup dark corn syrup
1   cup pecan pieces

Heat oven to 375 degrees. Combine eggs, sugar, salt, butter and syrup; beat thoroughly. Stir in nuts. Pour into pastry shell. Bake 40 to 50 minutes or until filling is set and pastry is browned. Cool.

SWEET POTATO PIE

     prepared 9" pastry shell
2   eggs
2   cups cooked & mashed sweet potato
¾   cup sugar
1   teaspoon cinnamon
½   teaspoon salt
½   teaspoon ginger
¼   teaspoon cloves
1⅔ cup evaporated milk (or light cream)

Heat oven to 425 degrees. In a mixing bowl, beat eggs lightly; mix in remaining ingredients and pour into pie shell. Bake 15 minutes. Reduce temperature to 350 degrees and bake 45 minutes more. Pie is done when knife inserted in center comes out clean.

BANANAS FOSTER

6	firm, ripe bananas
½	cup butter
½	cup brown sugar
½	teaspoon cinnamon
2	tablespoons lemon juice
2	tablespoons creme de cacao
⅔	cup rum
	vanilla ice cream

Peel and slice bananas in half lengthwise, and horizontally. In a chafing dish, melt butter; add sugar, stirring until blended. Add cinnamon.

Add bananas to sugar mixture, turning until golden brown. Add lemon juice and creme de cacao. Just before serving, heat rum and pour over bananas. Flame and serve over vanilla ice cream. Yield: 8 servings.

BREAD PUDDING

3	cups stale bread cubes
½	cup raisins
2	cups milk
2	eggs, slightly beaten
3	tablespoons melted butter
1	teaspoon vanilla
¾	cup sugar

Place the bread cubes in an 8x8x2-inch greased baking pan. Sprinkle the raisins on top. In a medium bowl, combine the milk, eggs, butter, vanilla and sugar. Pour into the baking pan, covering all bread cubes with mixture. Bake at 350 degrees for 45 minutes or until custard is firm. Yield: 6 servings.

CREAMY PECAN RICE PUDDING

3 cups cooked rice
3 cups milk
½ cup sugar
3 tablespoons butter or margarine
½ cup raisins
1 teaspoon vanilla extract
½ cup pecans

Combine rice, milk, sugar, butter and raisins. Cook over medium heat until thickened, about 30 minutes, stirring often. Add vanilla and blend gently. Pour into six individual serving dishes, set aside to cool.

Chop pecans semi-fine. Place in an ovenproof dish and bake in a 350 degrees oven for 5 to 10 minutes, or until golden. Pudding may be served warm or cold, with sprinkled pecans. Yield: 6 servings.

NEW BERN'S BAKED APPLES

6 baking apples
3 tablespoons sugar
¼ teaspoon cinnamon
1 tablespoon butter or margarine
¼ cup water
2 tablespoons chopped walnuts or pecans (optional)
2 tablespoons raisins (optional)

Preheat oven to 400 degrees. Prepare a baking pan large enough to hold apples, by lining it with aluminum foil. Wash and core apples; peel away outer skin ⅓ the way down. Place the apples in the baking dish. Dividing evenly, sprinkle sugar and cinnamon into center well of apples. Cutting the butter into chunks, do the same. If using nuts or raisins, add these to the well. Place a little water in the bottom of baking pan to help steam the apples. Bake uncovered till tender, about 45 minutes. Serves 6.

STRAWBERRY-PEACH TRIFLE

¼ cup strawberry jam
1   8-inch spongecake layer
1   package (3 ounce) instant vanilla pudding mix
2½ cups milk
¼   teaspoon almond extract
1   can (16 ounce) peach slices, drained
1   cup nondairy whipped topping
8   fresh strawberries for top
    mint leaves for garnish

Spread jam over cake layer; cut cake in 1-inch cubes. In a large bowl, combine pudding mix, milk and almond extract; whisk until consistency of a thin pudding.

In 1½ -quart bowl, fit half of cake cubes, jam side up. Top with half of peach slices. Spoon half of pudding on top. Repeat layering, ending with pudding. Place fresh strawberries on the top layer. Garnish with whipped topping and mint. Makes 8 servings.

Desserts

COINJOCK STRAWBERRY SHORTCAKE

4   cups strawberries, washed, hulled, and halved
6   tablespoons sugar
1½   cups flour
2   teaspoons baking powder
1   teaspoon salt
4   tablespoons butter, cut into small pieces
¾   cup milk
         whipped cream for topping

Place strawberries in a medium bowl, sprinkle with 5 tablespoons sugar; set aside to sweeten for 30 minutes at room temperature.

Preheat oven to 400 degrees. Sift flour, baking powder, salt, and 1 tablespoon sugar together into a bowl. Cut butter into flour mixture with a pastry cutter, until mixture resembles coarse crumbs; mix in milk. On a floured surface, shape dough into a biscuit 2" thick and 6" in diameter.

Bake on an ungreased cookie sheet until just golden, about 15 minutes.

Cool slightly, then slice in half horizontally. Place bottom half of biscuit on a serving plate, and spoon half the strawberries on top. Place top half on top of strawberries, topping with remaining strawberries. Top all with whipped cream, if desired. Yield: 4 servings.

NOTE: Biscuit mix may be made into 4 individual shortcakes, if desired.

CORNCAKE INLET CORNY POUND CAKE

¾ cup corn kernels (fresh or canned)
1 stick (½ cup) unsalted butter, softened
½ cup sugar
¼ cup plain yogurt
1 teaspoon vanilla
2 teaspoons freshly grated orange zest
3 large eggs
1 cup flour
¼ teaspoon salt

Preheat oven to 350 degrees. Lightly oil an 8½x4½x2½-inch loaf pan.

In a medium bowl, beat together with an electric mixer butter and sugar, until light and fluffy. Add yogurt, vanilla, and zest and beat until just combined. Add eggs, one at a time, beating after each addition. Beat in corn and add flour and salt, beating until just combined.

Spread batter evenly in pan and bake in middle of oven 1 hour, or until golden and knife comes out clean. (This cake will not rise). Makes 1 loaf.

EMERALD ISLE FUNNEL CAKES

2 eggs
1½ cups milk
2 cups all-purpose flour, sifted
1 teaspoon baking powder
½ teaspoon salt
cooking oil
powdered sugar (optional), cinnamon (optional)

Combine eggs and milk, beating until well blended.

Sift together flour, baking powder and salt. Add to egg mixture, and beat until smooth.

Heat cooking oil 1-inch deep in frying pan, electric skillet or deep fryer to 360 degrees. Cover the bottom of a funnel with finger, pour in ½ cup batter and release into hot oil in a spiral pattern. Fry until golden, turn with spatula and tongs; drain on paper towels.

Sprinkle with powdered sugar and cinnamon if desired.

HARKER'S ISLAND BROWNIES

½   pound butter
4   tablespoons cocoa
1   cup water
2   cups flour
2   cups sugar
1   teaspoon baking soda
½   teaspoon salt
½   cup buttermilk
2   eggs
1   teaspoon vanilla

Heat a small saucepan over medium heat. Melt butter, careful not to burn; add cocoa and water. Bring mixture to a boil. Remove from heat, keep warm.

In a mixing bowl, sift together flour, sugar, baking soda and salt. Add hot cocoa mixture and stir until just blended. Add buttermilk, eggs and vanilla. Stir until smooth. Pour into a greased 13x9-inch pan. Bake at 350 degrees for 15 to 20 minutes, or until firm. Allow to cool; using a sharp knife, cut brownies into squares. Yield: 24-36, depending on size of squares.

LEMON-GLAZED POPPY SEED CAKE

¼   cup poppy seeds
1¼ cups water
1   package yellow cake mix
¼   cup salad oil
3   eggs
3   tablespoons confectioners sugar
1   teaspoon lemon juice
1-2 teaspoons water

Preheat oven to 350 degrees. Soak poppy seeds in water for 30 minutes. Generously grease and flour an angel cake or bundt pan. In a large bowl, blend cake mix, oil, eggs, poppy seeds and water. Beat 4 minutes with an electric mixer at medium speed. Pour into cake pan. Bake 40-50 minutes or until cake springs back when touched lightly. Cool 10 minutes. Remove from pan, let cool completely, before applying glaze.

To glaze: in a small bowl, mix sugar with lemon juice and 1 teaspoon water. Whisk into a syrup-like glaze. Use more water if thinner glaze is desired. Drizzle lemon glaze over top of cooled cake. Yield: 8-10 servings.

After a cake comes from the oven, it should be placed on a rack for about five minutes. Then the sides should be loosened and the cake turned out on a rack to finish cooling.

Cakes should not be frosted until thoroughly cool.

MARION STATE BLACK FOREST CHEESECAKE

¾ cup chocolate graham cracker crumbs
2 (8-ounce) packages light cream cheese, softened
1½ cups sugar
¾ cup egg substitute
1 cup semi-sweet chocolate morsels, melted
¼ cup cocoa
1½ teaspoons vanilla extract
1 (8-ounce) container sour cream
1 (21-ounce) can cherry fruit filling
¾ cup light frozen whipped topping, thawed

Lightly grease a 9-inch springform pan. Sprinkle the chocolate cookie crumbs on the bottom. Beat cream cheese at high speed with an electric mixer until fluffy; gradually add sugar, beating well. Gradually add egg substitute, melted chocolate morsels, cocoa and vanilla extract. Stir in sour cream; pour into prepared pan.

Bake at 300 degrees for 1 hour and 20 minutes or until done. Remove from oven; run a knife around edge of pan to loosen sides. Cool on a wire rack; cover and chill at least 8 hours. Remove sides of springform pan, and spread cherry fruit filling over top of cheesecake. Serve with whipped topping. Yield: 12 servings.

VIRGINIA DARE SPONGE CAKE

6   egg yolks
½   cup orange juice
1½ cups sugar
½   teaspoon vanilla
1½ cups cake flour
¼   teaspoon salt
6   egg whites
¾   teaspoon cream of tartar

With an electric mixer at high speed beat egg yolks until thick and lemon-colored; add orange juice and continue beating until very thick. Gradually beat in sugar, then vanilla. Fold in flour, sifted with salt, a little at a time. In a separate smaller bowl, beat egg whites until foamy; add cream of tartar and beat until they form moist, glossy peaks. Fold egg whites into egg yolk mixture. Bake in a 10-inch ungreased angel cake pan at 325 degrees for 1 hour. Invert pan to cool. Yield: 8 servings.

WANCHESE ISLAND WACKY CAKE

1½ cups all-purpose flour
½   teaspoon salt
1   cup sugar
1   teaspoon baking powder
3   rounded tablespoons cocoa
1   tablespoon vinegar
1   teaspoon vanilla
5   tablespoons vegetable oil
1   cup cold water

Heat oven to 350 degrees. Grease and flour an 8-inch square pan. In a large mixing bowl, sift dry ingredients and mix. Make 3 wells in dry ingredients. Add vinegar to one, vanilla to another and oil to the third. Pour water over all and mix well. Pour into prepared pan. Bake 40 to 45 minutes or until done. Serves 6.

BENNE WAFERS, CHARLESTON STYLE

1   stick margarine
2   cups brown sugar
1   egg
1   cup plain flour
¼   teaspoon salt
½   teaspoon baking powder
1   teaspoon vanilla
⅔ to ¾ cups sesame seeds, toasted

Cream together margarine and sugar. Add egg, flour, salt and baking powder. Add vanilla and sesame seed. Drop wafer dough about ½ teaspoonful on greased cookie sheet. Bake at 325 degrees, 8 to 10 minutes. Allow to cool about 1 minute before removing from sheet. Yields over 100 wafers. Note: Wafers burn easily, so watch closely.

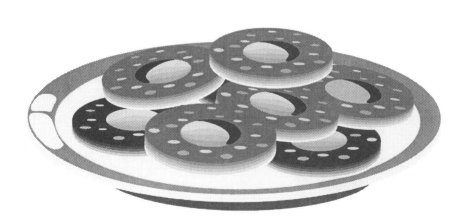

CALLAWASSIE PINA COLADA DROPS

1¼ cups all-purpose flour
½ teaspoon baking powder
¼ teaspoon salt
3 tablespoons unsalted butter
3 tablespoons margarine
½ cup granulated sugar
1 egg
½ teaspoon rum extract
¼ cup chopped glaceed pineapple
½ cup shredded coconut
   glaceed cherries for decoration

Stir together flour, baking powder and salt on a piece of waxed paper. Beat together butter, margarine and sugar in a bowl until creamy. Beat in egg and rum extract until well blended. Stir in flour mixture, pineapple and coconut. Shape into a ball; wrap in plastic wrap and refrigerate several hours or overnight.

Prior to baking, spray baking sheet with non-stick cooking spray. Drop rounded teaspoons of dough onto baking sheets. Top each cookie with half glaceed cherry. Bake at 350 degrees for 10 to 12 minutes. Cool on wire racks. Makes about 3 dozen cookies.

CHOCOLATE-PEANUT-BUTTER SQUARES

2   packages (10-ounce) peanut butter pieces
⅓   cup butter or margarine
2   cans (14 ounce) sweetened condensed milk
2   cups finely ground honey graham-crackers (15 crackers)
1½   cups unsalted peanuts, finely chopped
1   package (12 ounce) semisweet chocolate pieces

Line a 13x9x2-inch baking pan with foil. Melt peanut butter pieces and butter in small saucepan or bowl set over hot water until smooth. Spoon into large bowl. Whisk in sweetened condensed milk. Gradually stir in crumbs and ½ cup peanuts, using hands if necessary, to mix thoroughly. Pat the mixture evenly into the prepared pan. Refrigerate until firm, for about 30 minutes.

Melt chocolate pieces in small heavy saucepan set over very low heat, stirring occasionally, until smooth. Spread over top of peanut mixture. Sprinkle with remaining peanuts. Set aside until firm, about 3 hours. Cut into squares. Makes 3½ dozen.

GINGERBREAD ROUNDS

½ cup shortening
½ cup sugar
1 teaspoon baking powder
1 teaspoon ground ginger
½ teaspoon baking soda
½ teaspoon ground cinnamon
½ teaspoon ground cloves
½ cup molasses
1 egg
1 tablespoon vinegar
2½ cups all-purpose flour

In a mixing bowl, beat shortening with an electric mixer on medium to high speed 30 seconds. Add sugar, baking powder, ginger, baking soda, cinnamon, and cloves. Beat until combined, scraping bowl. Beat in the molasses, egg, and vinegar until blended. Beat in as much of the flour as you can with the mixer. Stir in remaining flour. Divide dough in half. Cover and chill for 3 hours or until easy to handle.

Preheat oven to 375 degrees and grease a cookie sheet; set aside. On a lightly floured surface, roll half of the dough at a time to a ⅛-inch thickness. Cut into cookies, using a 2½-inch round cutter. Place 1 inch apart on the prepared cookie sheet. Bake about 4 minutes or until done. Yield: about 48 cookies.

MANTEO'S OATMEAL RAISIN COOKIES

1	cup (2 sticks) butter or margarine, softened
1	cup firmly packed, brown sugar
½	cup granulated sugar
2	eggs
1	teaspoon vanilla
1½	cups all-purpose flour
1	teaspoon baking soda
1	teaspoon cinnamon
½	teaspoon salt
3	cups Quaker Oats, quick, uncooked
1	cup raisins

Heat oven to 350 degrees. Beat together margarine and sugars until creamy, in a large bowl. Add eggs and vanilla; beat well. In a smaller bowl, combine flour, baking soda, cinnamon and salt. Add combined flour to butter and sugar mixture. Mix well. Stir in oats and raisins; mix until well blended.

Drop by rounded tablespoons onto ungreased cookie sheet. Bake 10 to 12 minutes or until golden brown. Cool 1 minute on cookie sheet; remove to wire rack. Yield: about 4 dozen.

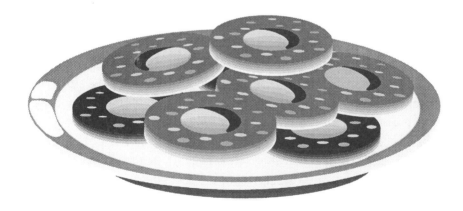

MEXICAN WEDDING COOKIES

½   cup unsalted butter
¼   cup powdered sugar
1   teaspoon vanilla
½   cup finely chopped or ground cashews (or other nuts)
1   cup flour
   additional powdered sugar for sprinkling

Cream butter and powdered sugar. Mix in the vanilla, nuts and flour. Wrap dough in plastic and chill until it is firm (at least 1 hour).
Preheat oven to 350 degrees. Pinch off dough and roll into balls about 1-inch in diameter. Place them on an ungreased cookie sheet and bake for about 18 minutes or until done. While still warm, coat or sprinkle cookies with additional powdered sugar. Store in an air-tight container. Yield: about 24 cookies.

PEANUT BLOSSOM COOKIES FROM PASQUOTANK

1   (14-ounce) can sweetened condensed milk
¾   cup creamy peanut butter
1   teaspoon vanilla extract
2   cups buttermilk biscuit & baking mix
⅓   cup sugar
1   (9-ounce) package milk chocolate kisses

Stir together milk, peanut butter, and vanilla, stirring until smooth. Add biscuit mix, stirring well. Shape dough into 1-inch balls; roll in sugar, and place on ungreased baking sheets. Make an indentation in center of each ball with thumb or spoon handle. Bake at 375 degrees for 8 to 10 minutes or until lightly browned. Remove cookies from oven and press a chocolate kiss in center of each cookie. Transfer to a wire rack to cool completely. Yield: 4 dozen.

Desserts

RODANTHE LEMONY RAISIN BARS

1½   cups raisins
1   (14-ounce) can sweetened condensed milk
1   tablespoon lemon juice
1   tablespoon grated lemon rind
1   cup butter or margarine, softened
1⅓   cups firmly packed brown sugar
1½   teaspoons vanilla extract
1   cup all-purpose flour
½   teaspoon baking soda
¼   teaspoon salt
2½   cups oats
¾   cup chopped walnuts

Heat oven to 375 degrees. In saucepan, combine raisins, sweetened condensed milk, lemon juice and lemon rind. Cook and stir over medium heat just until bubbly. Cool slightly.

In a bowl, combine butter, brown sugar and vanilla; beat well. Add flour, baking soda and salt; mix well. Stir in oats and walnuts.

Reserve 2 cups oat mixture for topping. Press remaining mixture into a 13x9-inch greased pan. Spread raisin mixture to within ½ inch of edges. Sprinkle with reserved oat mixture; press lightly.

Bake 25 to 30 minutes or until golden brown. Cool. Makes 48 bars.

SMITH ISLAND SUGAR COOKIES

1   cup butter, softened
1   cup sugar, divided
1   large egg
1   teaspoon vanilla extract
1¼   cups all-purpose flour
½   teaspoon baking powder

Beat butter at medium speed with an electric mixer until creamy; gradually add ¾ cup sugar, beating well. Beat in egg and vanilla. In another bowl, combine flour and baking powder; add to butter mixture, beating at low speed until blended. Shape dough into 1-inch balls; place on greased baking sheets. Dip a smooth-bottomed glass into remaining sugar, and flatten balls to ¼-inch thickness. Sprinkle remaining sugar over cookies.

Bake at 350 degrees for 12 to 14 minutes; transfer to wire racks to cool. Yield: 3 dozen.

SNICKERDOODLES

1   cup shortening
1½   cups sugar
2   eggs
2¾   cups sifted flour
2   teaspoons cream of tartar
½   teaspoon salt
1   teaspoon baking powder
For rolling:
2   tablespoons sugar
2   tablespoons cinnamon

Mix shortening, sugar and eggs. Sift dry ingredients together and gradually blend into sugar mixture. Roll into balls the size of walnuts. Roll balls in sugar and cinnamon mixture and place on ungreased cookie sheet. Bake 7 to 10 minutes at 400 degrees. Makes 4 dozen.

     Desserts

FUDGE FROM FRISCO

4½ cups sugar
1 (13-ounce) can evaporated milk
18 ounces semi-sweet chocolate pieces
½ pound butter
3 teaspoons vanilla
2 cups chopped pecans or walnuts

Combine sugar and milk in a saucepan. Bring to a boil and boil over medium heat for 6 minutes, stirring constantly. Remove from heat; add chocolate pieces, butter, vanilla and nuts; stir.

Spread mixture evenly on a greased 13x9-inch pan and allow to set up in a cool place for 6 hours. Cut into squares. Yield: 36-48 pieces, depending on size.

NORTH CAROLINA HOME-COOKED PEANUTS

2 cups raw shelled red skin or blanched North Carolina peanuts
1½ cups peanut oil or enough to cover peanuts

In an electric skillet, deep fryer or heavy saucepan heat oil to 350 degrees. Add peanuts and cook, stirring occasionally for about 5 minutes or until just under doneness desired (they continue to cook as they cool). Drain on paper towels and salt if desired.

For roasted peanuts (parched): place raw North Carolina peanuts in a shallow baking pan. Roast in a 350 degrees conventional oven - 15 to 20 minutes for shelled, 20 to 25 minutes for in-shell peanuts. Remove from heat just short of doneness. Cool.

PAWLEY'S ISLAND PECAN PRALINES

3	cups sugar
1	can (13 ounce) evaporated milk
2	cups whole pecans
2	tablespoons butter or margarine
2	teaspoons peanut butter
2	teaspoons vanilla

In a heavy saucepan, combine sugar, milk, pecans, butter and peanut butter; cook over low heat, stirring often. While candy is cooking, put newspaper with waxed paper on top of kitchen counter. Continue stirring, making sure candy does not scorch or burn. Cook 20 to 25 minutes, until candy reaches the softball stage. When candy makes a softball, remove pot from stove and add vanilla, stirring well. Drop by tablespoonfuls onto waxed paper and cool. Yield: 35 pralines.

SUNSET HARBOR SPICY WALNUTS

1 cup California walnut halves
1 teaspoon Old Bay Seasoning
1 teaspoon canola oil

In a medium bowl, mix together walnut halves, seasoning and oil. Line a cookie sheet with aluminum foil. Spread the seasoned walnuts evenly on the cookie sheet. Bake in a pre-heated 350 degrees oven, 25 -30 minutes.

Index

Index

Desserts

Meat

Poultry

Salads

Soups

Seafood

Vegetables

Notes

Notes

To order additional copies, make checks payable to:
Father & Son Publishing, Inc. and mail to:
4909 North Monroe Street • Tallahassee, Florida 32303

Please send me_____copies of **Beach Cuisine** @ $12.95 plus $3.00
each for postage and handling. Florida residents add 7% sales tax.
Enclosed is my check or money order for $ _____

Name _____

Address _____

City _____ State _____ Zip _____

Mastercard/Visa# _____

Exp. date _____ Signature _____

- -

To order additional copies, make checks payable to:
Father & Son Publishing, Inc. and mail to:
4909 North Monroe Street • Tallahassee, Florida 32303

Please send me_____ copies of **Beach Cuisine** @ $12.95 plus $3.00
each for postage and handling. Florida residents add 7% sales tax.
Enclosed is my check or money order for $ _____

Name _____

Address _____

City_____ State _____ Zip_____

Mastercard/Visa# _____

Exp. date_____ Signature_____

- -

To order additional copies, make checks payable to:
Father & Son Publishing, Inc. and mail to:
4909 North Monroe Street • Tallahassee, Florida 32303

Please send me_____ copies of **Beach Cuisine** @ $12.95 plus $3.00
each for postage and handling. Florida residents add 7% sales tax.
Enclosed is my check or money order for $ _____

Name _____

Address _____

City _____ State _____ Zip _____

Mastercard/Visa# _____

Exp. date _____ Signature _____

To order additional copies, make checks payable to:
Father & Son Publishing, Inc. and mail to:
4909 North Monroe Street • Tallahassee, Florida 32303

Please send me_____copies of **Beach Cuisine** @ $12.95 plus $3.00
each for postage and handling. Florida residents add 7% sales tax.
Enclosed is my check or money order for $ _____

Name _____

Address _____

City _____ State _____ Zip _____

Mastercard/Visa# _____

Exp. date _____ Signature _____

- -

To order additional copies, make checks payable to:
Father & Son Publishing, Inc. and mail to:
4909 North Monroe Street • Tallahassee, Florida 32303

Please send me_____ copies of **Beach Cuisine** @ $12.95 plus $3.00
each for postage and handling. Florida residents add 7% sales tax.
Enclosed is my check or money order for $ _____

Name _____

Address _____

City_____ State _____ Zip_____

Mastercard/Visa# _____

Exp. date _____ Signature _____

- -

To order additional copies, make checks payable to:
Father & Son Publishing, Inc. and mail to:
4909 North Monroe Street • Tallahassee, Florida 32303

Please send me_____ copies of **Beach Cuisine** @ $12.95 plus $3.00
each for postage and handling. Florida residents add 7% sales tax.
Enclosed is my check or money order for $ _____

Name _____

Address _____

City _____ State _____ Zip _____

Mastercard/Visa# _____

Exp. date _____ Signature _____